JK ROWLING
The Wizard Behind Harry Potter

JK ROWLING
The Wizard Behind Harry Potter

Marc Shapiro

JOHN BLAKE

Published by John Blake Publishing Ltd, 3 Bramber Court,
2 Bramber Road, London W14 9PB, England

First published in 2003

ISBN 1 84454 013 8

British Library Cataloguing-in-Publication Data: A catalogue record for this
book is available from the British Library.

Printed and bound in Great Britain by Bookmarque

1 3 5 7 9 10 8 6 4 2

Papers used by John Blake Publishing Ltd are natural, recyclable products
made from wood grown in sustainable forests. The manufacturing processes
conform to the environmental regulations of the country of origin.

Every attempt has been made to contact the relevant copyright-holders,
but some were unobtainable. We would be grateful if the appropriate
people could contact us.

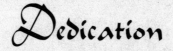 Dedication

To all the good people.
My wife, Nancy. My daughter, Rachael.
My mother, Selma. My agent, Lori.
Bennie and Freda. Keri, Bad Baby, Chaos.
Mike Kirby, Steve Ross.

And finally to JK Rowling for lighting up
the imagination of a whole generation.
All good thoughts to you.

Acknowledgements

Since *Harry Potter* burst on the scene, JK Rowling has been the subject of many press articles and has given many interviews. I found the following publications, with their high level of professionalism, particularly helpful: *Current Biography*, the *Daily Telegraph*, *Time*, *Newsweek*, *Entertainment Weekly*, the *Boston Globe*, *Salon* magazine, the *New York Times*, the *Guardian*, the *Los Angeles Times*, *School Library Journal*, *Book* and *People*.

The following websites also helped in this journey: *JK Rowling: Raincoast Kids*; *Meet JK Rowling: Scholastic.com*; *JK Rowling: Bookwire*; *The Unofficial Harry Potter Fan Club Page*; *Harry Potter: Scholastic.com*; *The Essential Harry Potter*; books: *BBC*

Dedication

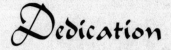

To all the good people.
My wife, Nancy. My daughter, Rachael.
My mother, Selma. My agent, Lori.
Bennie and Freda. Keri, Bad Baby, Chaos.
Mike Kirby, Steve Ross.

And finally to JK Rowling for lighting up
the imagination of a whole generation.
All good thoughts to you.

Contents

Acknowledgements

Since *Harry Potter* burst on the scene, JK Rowling has been the subject of many press articles and has given many interviews. I found the following publications, with their high level of professionalism, particularly helpful: *Current Biography*, the *Daily Telegraph*, *Time*, *Newsweek*, *Entertainment Weekly*, the *Boston Globe*, *Salon* magazine, the *New York Times*, the *Guardian*, the *Los Angeles Times*, *School Library Journal*, *Book* and *People*.

The following websites also helped in this journey: *JK Rowling: Raincoast Kids*; *Meet JK Rowling: Scholastic.com*; *JK Rowling: Bookwire*; *The Unofficial Harry Potter Fan Club Page*; *Harry Potter: Scholastic.com*; *The Essential Harry Potter*; books: *BBC*

INTRODUCTION

I LOVE TO READ

I confess, I love to read. After a hard day's work, there is no better way to wind down and relax than by curling up in a soft, comfortable chair, putting my feet up on an equally soft stool, and flipping through the pages of a good book as my cat, Chaos, purrs contentedly in my lap. What I read depends on what kind of mood I'm in.

Sometimes I want to find out about real people and real lives, so I will pick up a biography. But there are also those times when reading about the real world is the last thing on my mind. That is when I will pick up a science-fiction story, a spooky thriller, or a *Harry Potter* book – and escape to a place I've never been before.

There has always been a sense of comfort in escaping into a world of fantasy. Which is why the adventures of Harry Potter are so much fun for children and adults alike. There are, quite simply, no rules in a *Harry Potter* book – or at least none that cannot be broken in the name of fun and adventure.

We can have adventures in Harry's world that we cannot have anywhere else. As we flip through the pages of *Harry Potter and the Philosopher's Stone* or *Harry Potter and the Chamber of Secrets*, we can close our eyes and pretend we've just finished a rousing game of Quidditch and are now back in the hallowed halls of Hogwarts, learning the fine arts of charms, spells and magic, alongside good friends Ron and Hermione, at the feet of Professor Dumbledore.

Entering the world of Harry Potter is like following Alice down the rabbit hole into Wonderland. It is a place where just about anything can happen and usually does. Some of what goes on is truly frightening. I would not want to meet Voldemort or a Dementor on a dark night. But I sure would love to rip open a Howler and have it scream out its message to me. Travelling by way of Floo Powder would definintely beat being stuck in rush-hour traffic. And I doubt anyone could find a better friend than Ron or Hermione.

The sign of a good fantasy is when the reader can lose himself or herself in it. And it goes with out saying that millions of children and adults around the world have done just that through the adventures of Harry Potter.

But being curious, we also have questions.

How did the author come up with those ideas? What does the person who created Harry look like? What colour is her hair? After we have enjoyed our trip to fantasyland, we eventually want to know all about her.

What is the person who writes the *Harry Potter* stories like? Is she young or old? Happy or sad? Does she live alone, or does she write these fantastic stories with a brood of children underfoot? Did she have a happy childhood or was her family life so unhappy she was driven to escape into the world of fantasy?

Those were the questions I wanted to have answered. Which is why I set out to write *JK Rowling: Princess of Dreams*.

Often, the story behind the author is as interesting, if not more so, than what is written. In the case of JK Rowling, the story has a little bit of everything. There is happiness and love. There is also some sadness. The story of JK Rowling is also one of bravery, determination, and triumph over seemingly overwhelming odds.

And, finally, there is the happy ending. The life of JK Rowling sounds very much like the stories she writes and is, in a way, a fairytale come to life. Knowing about JK Rowling and how she came to write the most popular books in the whole wide world will not change your feelings about Harry Potter. But a closer look at the wizardry of Harry Potter's creator will definitely give you the story behind the story.

And knowing more will only add to the enjoyment the next time you sit in your chair or crawl into bed and pull the covers up tight and disappear into the land of Harry Potter one more time.

I am back to my comfortable chair and my good book.

Chaos is purring.

It is time to turn the page.

Marc Shapiro

1

WILD ABOUT HARRY

Sometimes the real world can be a confusing place. It is not always fair or kind. And in the real world there are not always happy endings. Which is why, every once in a while, we like to escape into the world of fantasy – a place where things always go our way and there is always a happy ending.

We want to believe in fantastic creatures in imaginary lands. We want to believe in magic powers, good friends and the power of good to triumph over evil. We all fantasize about being able to fly and lift buildings off the ground. And how good a magic sword would feel in our hand as we go off to slay a dragon or win the hand of a beautiful princess.

That is why we like Superman, Peter Pan, Mary Poppins and the amazing adventures of Frodo in *The Lord of the Rings*. And it is why we are all now Potterites who can't wait for the further adventures of our favourite wizard, Harry Potter, a 13-year-old English orphan who attends the Hogwarts School of Witchcraft and Wizardry and tries to be a normal boy while confronting the truly fantastic at every turn.

The author of the Harry Potter books, JK (Joanne Kathleen) Rowling, is a grown woman with a child of her own. She is sensible, modest, and realistic – all good qualities when it comes to being a good parent and a positive member of the real world. She likes to walk the streets of her home town of Edinburgh, Scotland. She will sit for hours in her favourite café, sipping an espresso and watching as the world passes her by.

But there is something that sets JK Rowling apart from the rest of us. For Joanne Kathleen Rowling likes to dream at all hours of the day and night. She dreams of faraway lands, larger-than-life good guys, truly evil bad guys, and likeable young children who try and make sense of it all. But unlike others, she turns her dreams into reality when she sits down with pen and paper and begins to write about the adventures of Harry Potter.

A smile crosses her face. Her already expressive eyes, framed by long wavy hair, grow even wider. Her pen slashes across the paper like a lightning bolt. In her mind, a door to a delightful new world of imagination and wonder has just opened wide and she is about to pass through it.

When JK Rowling sits down to give new life to Harry Potter, usually in her favourite writing place, a café called Nicholson's, a change comes over the author. Because to create the latest adventure of Harry, his good friends Ron Weasley and Hermione Granger, and their adventures, Joanne has to stop being an adult and become a child who also wants to believe in the unbelievable.

And once Joanne becomes that child, almost anything can and does happen.

From the opening passages of *Harry Potter and the Philosopher's Stone*, we can sense that something quite out of the ordinary is up. Our introduction to Harry is not a happy one. He is an orphan who has been living for ten years in a closet under the stairs of his cruel aunt and uncle's house. But we soon discover that Harry is not an ordinary soul. He is the son of wizards. However, Harry does not have a clue that he even has these powers until one day a giant appears out of nowhere and delivers to Harry a scholarship to the Hogwarts School of Witchcraft and Wizardry.

Once there, Harry discovers friends, foes, his magical powers and a mission to get rid of the evil that lies hidden in the depths of the school. In the classic sense, friends unite, evil is banished – at least temporarily – and all is well.

There is much more of the same in *Harry Potter and the Chamber of Secrets*, as a more mature Harry and his friends once again battle evil while the young wizard begins to learn more about his adopted land. And what he finds, thanks to Joanne's vivid imagination, are surprises around every corner. There is the diary that writes back, a dead professor who continues to teach class, and portraits of long-dead ancestors who come alive at night to primp and curl their hair.

By the third book, *Harry Potter and the Prisoner of Azkaban*, the author has seen fit to darken the tone. In the Dementors, we see truly disgusting evil. But Harry has by this time grown wise enough and powerful enough to fight the good fight. There is also that priceless moment when Harry discovers Cho Chan on the Quidditch field and thinks to himself that she is quite pretty.

Joanne has filled the pages of Harry's adventures with enticing images and has us hooked.

'I really can, with no difficulty at all, think myself back to 11 years old,' said Rowling in a *Time* magazine interview of her ability to tap into her own childhood when writing. 'I can remember being a kid and being very powerless and having this whole underworld that to adults is always going to be impenetrable. I think that I have very vivid memories of how it felt to be Harry's age.'

On more than one occasion, Joanne has acknowledged her childhood memories as an influence. For her, Hermione is very much herself as a child. And while there was no real-life Harry in her life, she has said that many elements of the character have come from people she knew. And her enemies? They spring to life when Joanne remembers the times when she had to face the school bully and did not know whether she would emerge unscathed.

The author has said that what she likes about writing the adventures of Harry Potter, and what brings her willingly to the task every day, is the notion of opening up a world of dreams and its possibilities.

'When you dream, you can do what you like,' she has told *Newsweek*.

And there have been dreams aplenty in the first five Harry Potter adventures; *Harry Potter and the Philosopher's Stone* (retitled *Harry Potter and the Sorcerer's Stone* in America), *Harry Potter and the Chamber of Secrets*, *Harry Potter and the Prisoner of Azkaban*, *Harry Potter and the Goblet of Fire* and *Harry Potter and the Order of the Phoenix*.

The world Harry Potter inhabits is dotted with strange creatures like Buckbeak, Scabbers and Crookshanks. There are good people like Professor Dumbledore and Hagrid and bad people like the Dursleys and the evil Lord Voldemort. In the world of Harry Potter, goblins run banks, apprentice students chase after balls on flying broomsticks, and wizards tread lightly as they enter the Forbidden Forest.

But finally it is Harry Potter, a skinny 13-year-old with glasses, green eyes and a head of unruly black hair who is the heart and soul of JK Rowling's adventures. The author feels that Harry is a mirror into her young readers' souls.

'Harry is smart and good at sports and a lot of things that other children would like to be,' Rowling once told an interviewer. 'But children also feel for him because he has lost his parents. If an author makes a character an orphan, few children will want to be an orphan, too. But it is a freeing thing because a certain weight of parental expectation is lifted.'

Yet the adventures of Harry Potter are much more than merely escapism for the preteen set. Adults have also taken Harry to their hearts and marvel at the simplicity and positive values presented in the tales. Harry is often the centre of a family's time together. Parents read to their children and children often read out loud to their parents. Or parents, after their children have gone to sleep, have been known to sit down with the book and read it themselves.

The author regularly reads her fan mail and is therefore well aware that the power of Harry Potter to capture readers has spanned the generations. A woman from Glasgow, Scotland, recently wrote to Joanne's British publisher asking how to go about joining the Harry Potter Fan Club, adding as an aside that she was 60 years old. An Englishman, when inquiring about the possibility of a Harry Potter movie, described himself as 'a child at heart, an adult in body'. She has had reports of family squabbles breaking out at bedtime when a parent wanted to finish reading a chapter and ended up taking the book from her children so she could read the book herself.

Joanne has thought long and hard about why people of all ages respond to Harry, and she thinks she knows the reason why.

'I think some of the reason is that Harry has to accept adult burdens in his life, although he is a child,' she said in a recent interview. 'There's something very endearing about that to kids and adults as well. Harry is also an old-fashioned hero. There's enough human frailty in Harry that people of all ages can identify with.'

The author also points to a sense of morality that runs through each book. Rather than preach, she gets her messages across quite naturally in the actions and thoughts of her characters. As we have discovered in the first four books, Harry

Potter is not the perfect little boy. He bends and breaks the rules when it suits his purpose and has all the insecurities of a normal boy or girl. Children and adults tend to love the fact that they can open a *Harry Potter* book and see themselves in the characters.

Arthur Levine, the US editor of the *Harry Potter* books, feels that a big attraction to readers is the idea of growing up under-appreciated, feeling like an outcast, and then suddenly bursting forth into the light and being discovered. 'That is the fantasy of every person who grows up smart but not very athletic. That's the emotional connection that drew me to the books,' he told the *New York Times*.

Whatever the reason, *Harry Potter* has become a worldwide phenomenon since the publication of the first book in 1997. To date, the first four books have sold more than 10 million copies in over 100 different languages. The books continue to reside at or near the top of a number of bestseller lists, and a movie studio recently announced that it will be making a big-budget movie of *Harry Potter and the Philosopher's Stone* in the not-too-distant future.

But there is more to the popularity of *Harry Potter* than book sales and movie deals. Kids have taken Harry to their hearts, and he has become a very real part of their playtime. They have made up games and put on plays centring around Harry and his adventures. Many of the numerous websites that have sprung up around the *Harry Potter* books feature original stories written by fans. Groups of children gather regularly to read *Harry Potter* out loud. One enterprising 11-year-old even had 'Educated at Hogwarts' printed up on business cards so he could hand them out to his friends.

Surprisingly, the author behind the fantastic adventures of Harry Potter is a person of relatively simple pleasures and tastes. She told an Internet site that she has no hobbies 'except hanging out with my friends and writing'. Her favourite holiday is Hallowe'en. Her favourite television shows are British comedies and the US imports *Frasier* and *The Simpsons*.

'I get bored with my life,' she once said. 'I prefer inventing things.'

But for Rowling, the true joy comes in the stories of how young children have embraced her tales. And they certainly have. A family in California was so anxious to read *Harry Potter and the Prisoner of Azkaban* that they ordered a British copy of the book on the Internet so that they would not have to wait months for the book to be published in America. When her third book went on sale at 3.45pm, a time when most English schools finish lessons for the day, she was amazed when stores sold out of every copy in a matter of minutes.

Rowling, who is often shy about doing interviews and has proven very secretive when asked about the further adventures of

Harry, came to enjoy book tours. In fact, she derives a lot of pleasure from book signings, when she gets to meet her young audience face-to-face. One example of this occurred during a visit to a school in England, when she was approached by a young boy carrying one of her books.

'He recited the first page of the first book to me from memory,' Rowling explained to *Newsweek*. 'When he stopped, he said, "I can go on." He continued reciting the first five pages of the book. That was unbelievable.'

However, she commented, one of her most gratifying moments came about during a reading and book signing appearance in Edinburgh.

'The event was sold out and the queue for signing at the end was very long. When a 12-year-old girl finally reached me, she said, "I didn't want there to be so many people here, because this is my book!" I told her that was exactly how I feel about my favourite books. Nobody else has a right to know them, let alone like them!'

What can best be described as Pottermania occurred last year when Joanne went to the USA on yet another book tour. Her many stops at bookstores across the country continued to amaze her and showed the author that while *Harry Potter* books are written in a distinctly British style, the messages in her books are international.

During a reading in a high school gymnasium in Santa Rosa, California, Joanne was shocked when she looked out and saw 2,500 *Harry Potter* fans jumping up and down in their seats and shouting, 'Harry! Harry!' at the top of their lungs.

The scene repeated itself in San Francisco, California, when Joanne's car rounded a corner and the writer was amazed to find more than 1,000 people standing in line in front of a bookstore for a 9.30am reading and autograph session. She would later discover that many of the children and their parents had spent the night queuing just so they could make sure they would get in for the event. One family had even made the six-hour trip by car from Los Angeles the night before just so they could be first in line. Joanne gave a short reading, answered her fans' many questions, and then signed 1,000 books in two hours. And then, quick as a flash, she was back inside her limo and gone.

'It was a little like having the Beatles here,' said an excited, out-of-breath bookstore representative to *Entertainment Weekly* after the event. 'Kids will probably be coming here for years saying, "Wow! That's where the *Harry Potter* lady was standing."'

For JK Rowling, the success of *Harry Potter* has been a fantasy all of its own. After years of struggling in unfulfilling jobs, living in poverty, and trying to make a go of it as a single mother, the author now lives comfortably in Scotland and regularly travels around the world. She has often reflected on how her reaction to the success of Harry 'has been shock' and that 'it was like being catapulted into fairyland'.

'I always find it difficult to be objective about Harry,' she once admitted to *BBC Online* when discussing the question of reality and fantasy in her books. 'To me, they remain my own private little world. For five years, they were my own private secret. From the moment I had the idea for the book, I could see a lot of comic potential in the idea that wizards walk among us.'

But, finally, JK Rowling's success is a dream come true. 'I would have been crazy to have expected what has happened to Harry,' she has said. 'The mere fact of being able to say I was a published author was the fulfilment of a dream I've had since I was a very young child.'

2

RABBIT AND MISS BEE

*J*K Rowling's parents met on a train in 1963. And, as in all good fairytales, it was love at first sight.

A quick glance at them, and Peter Rowling and his bride-to-be could not have been more different. Peter was the manager of an aircraft factory, while Ann worked as a lab technician. He came from a blue-collar world, while she was into books and more intellectual pursuits. However, none of those differences seemed to matter.

Because, as they courted, fell in love and eventually decided to get married, they discovered that they did indeed have a lot in common. They shared a good sense of humour, and both believed in the importance of home and family life. They also loved the English countryside and good books.

When they walked down the aisle, Peter and Ann felt that they had each found the perfect mate.

Shortly after their marriage, Peter and Ann moved into a small but comfortable home in the tiny hamlet of Chipping Sodbury. The couple loved the idea of living literally in the middle of England's famed forests and hillsides. But they had always been city dwellers, so they enjoyed their regular trips into the nearby town of Bristol, where they would shop and idle away the hours together. The young couple felt they had the perfect life. Only one thing could enrich their story.

And that came about in November 1965,

when the couple announced to family and friends that Ann was pregnant with their first child. The next nine months were a joyous and exciting time for Peter and Ann as they prepared for the arrival of their child. They speculated about whether their child would be a boy or a girl and discussed names for the child at great length. They regularly wandered into the room that had been picked out as the nursery and planned where the crib would be and what colours the walls should be painted. And as is true of all parents, they hoped that the child would be healthy and happy.

Late in July 1966, Peter's car pulled up in front of Chipping Sodbury General Hospital. It was time.

Joanne Kathleen Rowling came kicking and screaming into the world on 31 July 1966. In later years, Joanne would look back on the occasion of her birth as an omen of things to come. 'I think it is rather appropriate for someone who collects funny names to be born in a hospital named Chipping Sodbury,' she laughed.

Almost from the moment Joanne was born, Peter and Ann sensed the bright, inquisitive nature of their daughter. Her eyes were always wide in amazement at the world around her, and she was always grasping and touching things with curiosity. They could almost predict that one of the first words out of their daughter's mouth would be 'Why?'

Joanne once described her early childhood years as 'dreamy'. The young child seemed to have a knack for solitary pursuits. She often played imaginary games in her room or in the tall grass in her garden. If there was a tree around, she would climb it. If other children approached her, Joanne was quick to invite them to join her in any number of games. Even in those early years, she was very fond of the idea of 'let's pretend'.

Hoping to nurture Joanne's imagination,

her parents began reading to her at an early age. Because both parents were constant readers, it is no surprise that one of the author's earliest memories was of 'the house being full of books and of my parents constantly reading to me'. Joanne was fed a steady diet of fairytales and fantasy stories as well as a smattering of the classics. Even during her most uncomfortable moments, the sounds of her parents reading to her always had a calming effect.

'My most vivid memory of childhood is my father sitting and reading *The Wind in the Willows* to me,' she told the *Daily Telegraph*. 'I had the measles at the time, but I don't really remember that. I just remember the book.'

What her parents did not realise was that a constant exposure to literature – in particular, to fairytales and stories of the fantastic – had made an enormous impression on the young child. She began to dream up fantastic, well-plotted stories with larger-than-life characters.

When she was at play, her stories were full of character and detail, light-years beyond those generally produced by a child of her age.

Although she was too young to think in terms of what she wanted to be when she grew up, Joanne Kathleen Rowling, at a very early age, had this image of herself as somebody who would put pencil to paper and create magic worlds. 'Writing for me has always been a kind of wonderful compulsion,' she said in a 1999 interview. 'I don't think anyone could have made me do it or could have prevented me from doing it. It's weird, but writing is all I ever wanted to do.'

But these were private thoughts for Joanne, that wonderful secret that kept her warm and cosy in her bed at night and helped her to glide through her days. To tell even her parents would have ended all the fun.

But when her younger sister, Di, born less than two years after Joanne, reached three years old, five-year-old Joanne began making up tall tales about fantastic creatures and imaginary places and telling them to Di.

These stories would often centre on rabbits because, as Joanne has recalled, 'we badly wanted a rabbit'. One of the most memorable of these early flights of fantasy, and the one that always had Di roaring with little-girl laughter and excitement, was a story about how Di had fallen down a rabbit hole one day and ended up being fed strawberries by the rabbit family.

More often than not, Di would sit enthralled by her older sister's tales. She would inevitably ask Joanne to tell her the same story again and again, and because the stories were not written down, they would often come out slightly different in the retelling. Joanne was encouraged by her younger sister's response to begin jotting her stories down on paper. So, one day, not long after she turned six, Joanne sat down with pencil and paper and wrote her first story.

Not surprisingly, it was a story about a rabbit called Rabbit, who caught the measles and was visited by a number of friends, including a giant bee named Miss Bee.

'I wrote stories about rabbits for a couple of years. I definitely had a rabbit fixation,' Joanne once told an interviewer.

Di was thrilled with the story. Joanne's parents, who had taken to eavesdropping on their daughter's fantasies, were amused by their daughter's imagination but did not feel it necessary to involve themselves actively in any way. Their encouragement would have been superfluous anyway, because Joanne had already made up her mind that she was going to be a writer.

'Ever since Rabbit and Miss Bee, I knew I wanted to be a writer,' she told *School Library Journal*. 'I cannot overstate how much I wanted that. But I would rarely tell anyone so. I just never really spoke about it because I was embarrassed, and because my parents were the kind of parents who would have thought, Ah yes, that's very nice, dear. But where is the pension plan?'

Joanne grew into a bright child whose imagination was often the talk of the neighbourhood. This talent was also a topic during her first years at school, when her teachers would marvel at the maturity and creativity of her early stories and essays. Joanne took these early compliments as a sign that she had found something she was good at.

Another one of the young girl's early attempts at storytelling was a story of chills and adventure called *The Seven Cursed Diamonds*.

'At that age, I thought it was a novel,' she would recall in later years. 'But I think now that it was only a very long short story.'

And Joanne enjoyed more than just writing her own stories during those early years; her parents usually found her nose buried in the stories of others. The young child was quite outgoing and had a number of friends in the neighbourhood, but always seemed to prefer going off by herself and reading. Among her favourites was *The Little White Horse* by Elizabeth Goudge, *Manxmouse* by Paul Gallico, and the Narnia books by CS Lewis.

'I adored E Nesbit,' Joanne once said of her reading habits. 'I think her books are wonderful. I also liked Noel Streatfield, who did those girly books about ballet shoes and things. Even now, if I was in a room with one of the Narnia books, I would pick it up and re-read it like a shot,' she explained to the *Daily Telegraph*.

Shortly after Joanne began to write, her parents decided that they needed a bigger home and moved the family to the small town of Yate, just outside Bristol. Less than a year after that move, Peter and Ann decided that they liked the scenery better on the other side of Bristol and moved the family to yet another small town – Winterbourne.

Joanne and Di quickly adjusted to the moves and made friends easily with the local children. Winterbourne, in particular, was home to a lot of children Joanne and Di's age; they were immediately welcomed into the informal gang that would play games up and down the streets of the town. In those days, Joanne was very much a tomboy, engaging in just about every rough-and-tumble game without worrying about falling over and hurting herself. Even at that age, Joanne was not what you would call athletic and would often fall. But her willingness to have a go soon gained her the respect of her new friends.

Two of her closest friends in Winterbourne were a brother and sister named Ian and Vikki Potter. In later years, Ian Potter would tell *Book* magazine that when his sister and he would get together with Joanne and Di, they would occasionally tell stories.

'But most of all we liked dressing up and, nine times out of ten, it would be Joanne who would say, "Oh, let's play witches and wizards."'

Joanne remembered being quite close to Ian and Vikki during their days in Winterbourne. One reason for their friendship was their name.

'Their surname was Potter,' she once recalled. 'I always liked the name.'

3

CHILDISH THINGS

Shortly after Joanne Kathleen Rowling's ninth birthday, her parents decided it was time to move once again. Only this time it was because her parents' dream had finally come true.

Peter and Ann Rowling had both been born and raised in London and were basically city folk at heart. But because it was cheaper to live in the country, they had postponed any notion of living in a city. However, as Peter gained promotion at his car factory and began receiving a higher salary, the couple decided it was time to make the move.

The couple, despite their yearning for city life, had grown to enjoy the proximity of the countryside. Rather than a big city, the Rowlings decided smaller would be better.

Tutshill is a small town situated near Chepstow in the Forest of Dean. It was very much a bustling town with streets, stores and schools. But the river Wye ran through it and there were fields all around, making it the ideal mixture of city and country.

Joanne and Di quickly adjusted to their new surroundings. They would frolic for hours by the river and make up fantasy games to act out in the fields. Joanne was outgoing and soon made friends in her neighbourhood. When she felt comfortable enough, she would bring out some of her stories and read them to the local kids.

While the other children did not quite know what to make of this little girl who used big words and told funny stories about fantastic places, they were impressed and gladly made room for a regular storytime from Joanne.

She would continue to enjoy playground activities, but reading and writing, which are solitary pursuits, remained first on her list of passions.

When it came to books, she was already reading well beyond her class at school. At nine years old, Joanne discovered Ian Fleming's James Bond novels, and they became a regular part of her reading list.

Not too long after that, she discovered the works of Jane Austen and was never the same again. Austen's delicate passages and detailed stories became a model for Joanne Rowling. 'Jane Austen is my favourite author ... ever.'

There was only one drawback to living in the town of Tutshill – Joanne had to go to

Tutshill Primary School, and she hated it.

'It was a very small, very old-fashioned place,' she painfully remembered for the *Okubooks* website. 'The rolltop desks still had inkwells.'

But that was not the only problem Joanne had with the school. There was a new teacher to deal with. And this teacher scared the life out of Joanne. She was a strict, no-nonsense type who taught her class according to the book. Unfortunately for Joanne, the teacher's book and her new student did not agree when it came to certain subjects.

'She gave me a test on the very first morning and, after a huge effort, I managed to get zero out of ten,' she said.

On her first day, the teacher sat Joanne in a row of desks to the far right of the classroom. The young child was fine with that until a few days later when she figured out, by talking to her fellow students, that the teacher had put her in the 'stupid' row.

It seemed that the teacher had made up her seating chart based on how clever she thought her students were. The brightest students sat on the left side of the room and the rest sat on the right. Joanne painfully recalled her first days at Tutshill Primary when, she wrote, 'I was as far right as I could get without sitting on the playground.'

It was a tough first year for Joanne. She was not making friends as easily as she had in the past. Physically and emotionally she was changing. It all added up to a rough beginning at her new school.

'I wasn't as clever as I thought I should be,' she confessed when looking back on those days for *Salon* magazine. 'I don't think I was a know-all. I was obsessed with achieving academically, but that masked a huge insecurity. I think it is very common for plain young girls to feel this way. I definitely would not want to go back and do childhood again. I don't look back on it as a phase of blissful happiness at all.'

She was the new kid in school, and she had to deal with the embarrassment of being identified as 'dumb'. But Joanne managed to turn the experience around.

She studied hard and managed to make a small but loyal circle of friends. Not surprisingly, English was her best subject. Although she continued to write fantasy fables in her spare moments, she was not comfortable with sharing them with anyone but Di and one or two of her closest friends.

Joanne was determined to prove her teacher's impression of her wrong. By the end of the year, she had convinced the teacher that she was not by any means 'slow'. One day she was rewarded when her teacher told her she could now sit on the left side of the classroom. Joanne recalled the promotion with mixed emotions.

'I had been promoted to second left. But the promotion was at a cost. My teacher made me swap seats with my best friend. So in one short walk across the room, I became clever but unpopular,' Joanne recalled.

Joanne regained her popularity and continued through her primary school years in an uneventful way. Her grades continued to be good. She remained painfully shy, with only a small circle of close friends. And writing continued to be her passion.

No matter how busy her days were, she always managed to find some quiet time to release her fantasies. Her stories, full of magic and strange characters with funny names, were the highlight of her sister's playtime. The praise Joanne received from Di and her parents convinced Joanne, even as young as she was, that she would one day be an important writer and would live a wonderful, fairytale life.

Joanne successfully graduated from Tutshill Primary and was soon on her way to Wyedean Comprehensive School. The confidence and positive self-image that Joanne had fought hard to cultivate throughout her junior school disappeared during her first year at Wyedean.

She became insecure at the prospect of attending school with older children, and she was going through puberty and thus felt very self-conscious. It also did not help that she wore glasses. 'I was quiet, freckly, short-sighted and rubbish at sports,' she commented.

But Joanne managed to find her niche at Wyedean. Eventually, she found other girls like her – quiet, smart and on the fringes of being popular – and she became a part of that group. She did quite well at school, with English and foreign languages being her favourite subjects.

The youngster slowly began to come out of her shell at Wyedean. She was continuing to write and finally felt confident enough to risk it all by reading some of her stories to her new friends. They liked what they heard and were regularly entertained by Joanne's creative efforts.

'I used to tell my equally quiet and studious friends long serial stories during lunchtime,' she wrote in an essay. 'They usually involved us all doing heroic and daring deeds we certainly would not have done in real life.'

Joanne breezed through her comprehensive school years on a steady course with relatively few noteworthy achievements. There was the embarrassment of breaking her arm one day while playing the non-contact sport of netball. There was also the day Joanne finally came of age at school when she was attacked by the toughest girl in her year. She would later recall that she would logically have preferred to run from trouble rather than stand and fight. But fight back is exactly what she ended up doing.

'I didn't have a choice,' she said. 'It was hit back or lie down and play dead. For a few days, I was quite famous because she hadn't managed to flatten me. The truth was, my locker was right behind me and it held me up.'

Unfortunately, Joanne's new-found reputation as a tough girl lasted only a short time. She soon reverted to timidity and would spend weeks peering nervously around corners, in constant fear of being ambushed.

Through her later years at the comprehensive school, Joanne began to come out of her shell. Her confidence growing, she was now quicker to speak up in class and was more assertive in social conversations and activities. While still what would be considered very unathletic, she was now more inclined to assert herself with the other girls. This, she would later report, was due in part to the fact that her glasses had been replaced by contact lenses, so she was less fearful of being hit in the face.

In fact, Joanne, by her own reports, flowered in her teen years. She felt that, personally and socially, things had actually begun to get better and she finally came to the all-important realisation that there was more to Joanne Kathleen Rowling than someone who was driven to get everything right. Joanne was suddenly much more comfortable with herself.

Like most teenagers, Joanne had a growing sense of independence; this would lead to the occasional row with her parents, usually short-lived arguments over trivial matters. Her relationship with Di remained close. When not helping her younger sibling with her homework, Joanne would continue to use Di as her first audience for the many stories she was continuing to write. The second group to hear her latest tales was her girlfriends at school.

Despite the fact that she had numerous teachers who saw something in her and encouraged her in a creative direction, writing remained a largely private pursuit. The stories she felt confident enough to share were often the tales of action and adventure that featured herself and her friends as thinly-disguised characters in stories of derring-do.

Her other stories, those she perceived as more intimate, she would not show to anyone. These were the stories that she felt a real writer would write. And she was not quite ready to let the outside world into that part of her creative life.

Joanne's love for reading continued to blossom as well. She had long since begun to read about the lives of real people and had developed a particular infatuation for the author Jessica Mitford, a feminist who ran off and joined the Spanish Civil War at 19 and was a passionate supporter of human rights.

'I remember reading the book *Hons and Rebels* at 14, and it changed my life.'

Joanne had grown into quite the confident student in her senior year at Wyedean Comprehensive. She was popular and outgoing, and her grades were quite good. So good, in fact, that Joanne was appointed Head Girl in her final year.

Head Girl was a lofty position to which all the girls aspired. But, in fact, very little responsibility was attached to the role. Once a year, when some dignatory from the region came to visit the school, it was the job of the Head Girl to show her around the school fair. The requirement that Joanne dreaded the most was that the Head Girl also had to give a talk to the whole school.

'I decided to play them a record to cut down on the time that I had to speak to them,' she laughingly recalled. 'Well, the record was scratched, and right in the middle of playing, it began skipping and played the same line over and over again. Finally, the Deputy Headmistress came out on stage and kicked it.'

Joanne ended her years at Wyedean Comprehensive with high honours. Her teachers were predicting a bright future for her. Her parents were proud. Joanne

Kathleen Rowling was quiet on the subject of her future. She knew in her heart of hearts what she wanted to do with her life. She had her own hopes and dreams.

Now all she had to do was figure out how to make them come true.

4

LIFE LESSONS

Joanne wanted to write. But being admittedly 'the most disorganised person in the whole world', she did not know how to begin. So she would write something, read through it, and usually find enough fault in her work to discard it. Even when she was happy with a story, it still remained her own private happiness.

She had boxes and folders full of short stories, but did not have a clue how one went about getting them published. She knew magazines bought such stories all the time but never saw fit to submit one. Even thinking about doing so usually ended up with Joanne backing down in the face of her old fears of letting other people judge her work.

So, like so many others, Joanne was an 18-year-old with definite ideas but lacking the courage to carry them out. This was a side of herself that Joanne did not particularly like, and she would often upbraid herself for being too cowardly to challenge herself. But the truth was that Joanne Kathleen Rowling was just not ready to take on the world.

Because Joanne was frustrated at her inability to take that next big step in her writing life, she was easily influenced by others. Consequently, she was willing to take her parents' advice.

Peter and Ann, having not been privy to her writing ambitions, had long been bewildered at their eldest daughter's seeming lack of direction. Joanne's parents had regularly suggested that with her love of language, their daughter should study French and literature, which would lead to a wonderful career as a bilingual legal secretary. And with her good grades, they felt Exeter University would be the ideal place for her to go.

Joanne's heart, though, was in her writing and she felt that pursuing any other line of work would be a mistake. However, being an obedient child, Joanne reluctantly took her parents' advice and was soon enrolled at Exeter.

The teenager was encouraged by the stories she had heard that Exeter was a liberal establishment that was big on unconventional ideas. She figured that, if nothing else, she would find much to influence her in her true passions. In fact, what she discovered shortly after enrolling was that Exeter was actually quite conservative, wrapped up in traditional ideals.

'It was fantastic,' she told a reporter, 'but it did not offer quite the chance to be a radical that I planned.'

Joanne's years at Exeter were productive. She found that she was able to master French fairly easily. A big part of her education at Exeter was a year spent in Paris, learning to use the French language in a practical setting. Joanne found the year abroad exhilarating.

She took in the sights and marvelled at being in another country for the first time without her family. Joanne grew up during that year in Paris. By the time she returned to Exeter, Joanne Kathleen Rowling had grown confident in her ability to make her way in the world.

During this time, Joanne had her first serious relationship. Being in love and having someone care about her was an important thing for her. Joanne revelled in the fact that she was, in fact, attractive enough and bright enough to gain the affections of a loving partner.

Of course, every spare moment was taken up with writing. There was the usual batch of short stories that only a handful of people ever saw. She also attempted a novel. But while she was confident in other areas, Joanne steadfastly refused to submit any of her stories, belittling them whenever anyone would suggest that her stories were good and that she should send them out.

This lack of confidence in the thing she valued most haunted her every waking hour. In her heart, Joanne knew that it was time to shake off the doubts. Unfortunately, her head still had a firm hold on her fears and insecurities. So she continued to do nothing at all.

Joanne graduated from Exeter with honours and, as often happens, she and her boyfriend naturally drifted apart. But Joanne had little time to grieve over a lost love. She was soon doing the rounds of her first job interviews.

Getting dressed up and presenting herself at job interviews was not something the young woman liked doing. It seemed like a silly, unnecessary game. It made her feel totally inadequate and very much like a little girl again. Besides, this was not what she really wanted to do, which was to write fabulous stories, see them published, be able to keep writing and live happily ever after. But since she was not willing to take the risks necessary to reach that pinnacle, Joanne had to contend with the real world.

The next six years were a rough introduction to the often tedious life of the workaday world. Joanne went through a series of jobs. In one instance, she spent two years researching human rights violations for Amnesty International. While she felt she was doing important work and that her idol, Jessica Mitford, would approve, the work itself soon became predictable and boring, two things Joanne could not abide.

For the most part, she undertook a seemingly endless string of boring secretarial jobs. The work did not interest her and she was not making a lot of money. Additionally, as she has readily admitted, 'I later proved to be the worst secretary ever.'

Her mind always seemed to be on something else. 'Whatever job I had, I was always writing like crazy,' she confided. 'All I ever liked about offices was being able to type up stories on the computer when no one was looking. I was never paying much attention in meetings because I was usually scribbling bits of my latest stories in the margins of the pad or thinking up names for my characters. This is a problem when you're supposed to be taking the minutes of the meeting.'

Needless to say, Joanne's employers frowned on her writing fantasy stories during company time, and she was dismissed from a couple of her jobs. But for the most part, Joanne simply got tired of doing work she detested and would eventually quit. Well into her twenties, the young woman was like a boat without a rudder.

Joanne's parents were supportive but concerned that their eldest daughter seemed to be having trouble finding her place in life. Her only solace in an otherwise bleak world was her writing.

'I was writing a lot of short stories and a lot of started and abandoned novels,' she told *School Library Journal*. 'I felt I worked very hard and had served my apprenticeship in terms of writing.'

She felt less than positive about herself when those works would inevitably end up in a box with all the other stories that had not seen the light of day.

Unfortunately, all the hard work still did not add up to much, so Joanne reluctantly searched for yet another job. This time she found employment as an office worker for the Manchester Chamber of Commerce.

Joanne had another reason for going to Manchester. She had received a letter from her old boyfriend at Exeter, stating that he was in Manchester and that he'd like to see her again. The job she got was as dull and boring to her as all the others had been, but this time she was determined to make a go of things.

Joanne made time for her old boyfriend but remained diligent in her writing. At lunchtime, she would make her way to one of the nearby pubs or cafés, settle at an out-of-the-way table, and write. While far from anti-social, she would often find herself praying that nobody in the office was having a birthday or some other celebration that would require her to join in, taking up her precious writing time.

Joanne looked upon the travelling between London and Manchester as her private time. She would often while away the time reading a book, working on her latest story, or simply staring out of the window at the passing scenery. One day, as she returned to London after yet another day of unrewarding work, the train suddenly ground to a halt.

There was some kind of mechanical problem that, it was announced, would require a delay of about four hours. Normally this would have been ideal. But since Joanne was too tired to either read or write, she focused her attention on a group of cows, grazing in a meadow in front of her.

What she did not realise was that her life was about to change.

'I was sitting on the train, just staring out the window at some cows – it was not the most inspiring subject – when all of a sudden the idea for Harry just appeared in my mind's eye. I can't tell you why or what triggered it. But I saw the idea of Harry and the wizard school very plainly. I suddenly had this basic idea of a boy who didn't know what he was,' she remarked.

Joanne was enthralled with the vision that had come to her. She immediately reached for a pen and paper to begin jotting down notes and thoughts. Unfortunately, Joanne had neither. And so, with nothing but her memory to serve her, she sat quietly and just played with the notion of characters, funny names, and story possibilities.

By the time her train stopped at King's Cross station in London, Joanne had laid down the basic premise of the first *Harry Potter* story. Over the next few weeks and months, Joanne put every free moment into jotting down ideas and stories based on this imaginary boy and his adventures in a world ruled by magic. The *Harry Potter* files soon filled one box, then several.

Joanne continued her job at the Manchester Chamber of Commerce but took every opportunity before, during, and after work to fashion a single storyline for the first *Harry Potter* book. Soon, she came up with Harry, an orphan, being raised by a cruel aunt and uncle. He then finds out he is a wizard and is whisked off to a boarding school for young wizards called Hogwarts.

Joanne would often find herself smiling as she devised adventures for Harry and unusual names for the characters who would populate his world. Her whole outlook improved once she was inspired by Harry. Her parents and sister noticed the change, but they knew little about its cause. Joanne dropped little hints about something she was working on but stopped short of revealing the details. She felt that to let too much out would blunt the magic.

Joanne Kathleen Rowling was already thinking like a resident of Harry Potter's world.

But this period of good spirits would be short-lived. Her mother, who had been diagnosed with multiple sclerosis in the previous year, died suddenly at the age of 45.

Joanne was devastated. She was well aware that her mother had been ill but had no idea that MS would take her so quickly, and she felt terribly guilty that she had not been there in her mother's final hours. Her deepest regret was that she had never let her mother read any of Harry.

In her distracted state of mind, the young girl had a tough time concentrating on work, so soon afterwards, Joanne lost her job at the Manchester Chamber of Commerce.

'It was a nightmare period,' sighed Joanne. She told *People* magazine that writing about Harry was the only thing that got her through it.

5

HARRY IS BORN

*J*oanne was in an emotional turmoil. She had just turned 26. She was once again out of work, and the relationship with her boyfriend seemed to be going nowhere. And she felt consistently depressed and upset because of the death of her mother.

The only real joy in Joanne's life was Harry Potter. She had continued to work diligently on his adventures, with boxes overflowing with ideas, names and fragments of stories. Joanne was feeling confident about what she had jotted down and began seriously contemplating writing the novel. But she was torn between living out her dream of a life dedicated to writing and the guilt she was feeling at not being like everyone else.

Joanne was thinking very hard about what her life was about and what she wanted to do with it. One of the bright spots she kept coming back to was that year she had spent in Paris working as an assistant teacher. She had enjoyed it and thought she might enjoy it again. In any case, she felt she needed to do something constructive with her life.

Joanne's dreams of teaching in some far-off land finally won out. In September 1990, she announced to her family and friends that she would no longer settle for menial office work and soon accepted the offer of a job abroad, teaching English as a second language at a school in the northern Portuguese town of Oporto. Joanne was both excited and frightened at the prospect of going so far away to work, but she felt that being away from home and family was the only way she would ultimately find herself.

So she packed her bags, many of which contained her notes on Harry, kissed her father and sister goodbye and promised them she would write on a regular basis. Before she knew it, she was on her way.

Although she was homesick, Joanne quickly adjusted to life in Portugal. She immediately found a comfortable apartment and became well acquainted with the country, its people and its customs. She loved walking the quaint streets, window shopping and coming to terms with some of the more unusual Portuguese delicacies, such as tripe (the stomach lining of a cow). The people were friendly and it was sunny and warm all the time, a real contrast to the gloomy, cold weather in London. After a short while, the homesickness disappeared and Joanne settled into her teacher role.

Joanne's students took an immediate liking to her. And when they were not making fun of her name, calling her 'Rolling Stone', they would sit in rapt attention as Joanne taught them the fine art of speaking English. The transplanted Londoner was happy with the progress her students were making and proud of the good notices she had been receiving from the school superiors. She was also happy that her schedule allowed her to continue to write. 'I worked afternoons and evenings,' she recalled, 'and so I had my mornings free to write.'

Harry and his adventures at Hogwarts were slowly but surely coming together. The first pages of the novel were written on a wave of excitement. Joanne was discovering Harry much in the manner that her creation was discovering his magic – in short bursts of enthusiasm that often had her breaking into a spontaneous grin as the words flowed from her mind to the page.

She would chuckle as the names Hermione, Ron, Hagrid and Dumbledore instantly became immortalised in the shapes of Harry's many fantastic friends. Naming her characters was one of the most enjoyable parts about writing Harry. Having long been a collector of unusual names and clever when it came to creating her own, Joanne would often laugh uncontrollably when the likes of a Every Flavour Beans or a Justin Finch Fletchey would spring spotaneously to mind.

'Having a child who escapes the confines of the adult world and goes somewhere where he has power really appealed to me,' the author once revealed to the *Boston Globe* of her feelings while writing the first *Harry Potter* book. 'There's always room for a story that can transport readers to another place.'

But the excitement was often tempered by the frustration of trying to get everything about Harry and his world just right. The author admitted to some tears in those early days when, in detailing Harry's life as an orphan, she was forced to deal with the passing of her own mother.

Evil was also a notion that Joanne had to deal with when creating the villainous Lord Voldemort. Rather than create baddies typical of a children's book – noisy but not truly evil – she decided that evil in the world of *Harry Potter* would ring true to readers only if it was serious and its consequences befell the characters that the readers loved.

Ultimately, one aspect that caused Joanne the most concern was the tone of the books. From the beginning, Joanne was torn between writing the typical children's book, which often condescended to the reader, or simply writing the book that she would choose to read as an adult. Joanne chose the latter course.

Writing this book, despite the obstacles and challenges involved, was a constant joy

– one that would help her through her occasional bouts of loneliness. Joanne was friendly and outgoing with her co-workers but had remained reserved and shy around men. Despite having had a boyfriend at Exeter University, she had never thought of herself as pretty and so had never been too concerned that the years were rolling by without the prospects of a husband or a family in her life.

But all of that changed the day Joanne Kathleen Rowling fell in love.

She met him by chance. He was a journalist for one of the leading television stations in Portugal. Joanne, blushing like a schoolgirl, had been instantly attracted to his bright smile and his dark good looks. As they began to see each other, Joanne also discovered that he was bright, sensitive and interested in her.

Theirs was a whirlwind courtship. Within months of their meeting, Joanne and her handsome Portuguese lover were married.

The first two years of their marriage were good, if somewhat hectic, times for the couple. Her husband's work often kept him out until all hours and, with her schedule, they often found it difficult to find private time together. Still, Joanne found inspiration in her happiness, and it showed in her enthusiasm for her work and the continued progress of *Harry Potter*.

What had started out as a simple tale for young children was becoming more complex. What was intended as a book for young people was beginning to take on layers of depth equally suitable for adult readers. The characters were living and breathing in a very real way; although children, they were making difficult decisions and behaving much more maturely than most characters in children's stories. And so it did not bother Joanne when Harry's adventures in Hogwarts developed, with no end in sight.

In 1992, Joanne discovered that she was

pregnant. The young couple were thrilled and, privately, the mother-to-be hoped that the prospect of a baby in the house would help their relationship, which had hit a rough patch.

Sadly, the pressures of married life, coupled with all the physical and emotional demands of the pregnancy, soon began to weigh on Joanne. In her mind, her husband was always at work and was not showing her the same consideration she had first experienced. Joanne would often lapse into fits of depression. There were tears. Her husband did his best to comfort her, but to no avail. Unfortunately, the birth of the couple's daughter, Jessica, in 1993, did little to save the crumbling marriage.

'I was very depressed,' Joanne remembered painfully in a *UK News* interview. 'And having a newborn child made it doubly difficult. I simply felt like a non-person. I was very low and I felt I had to achieve something.'

In a matter of weeks, Joanne and her husband divorced. She has been rather secretive about her marriage, refusing to reveal the name of her husband or the actual reason for the divorce. She would only concede that 'I've made my mistakes in that area. Just because you've got a good brain doesn't mean you're any better than the next person at keeping your hormones under control.'

Joanne found herself in a terrible state. She felt there was no reason to stay in Portugal, where the memory of her failed marriage would continue to haunt her and her prospects for any kind of life as a recently divorced woman with a child were limited. She was prepared to return to London, although the idea of returning home as a divorced single mother was not something she was looking forward to doing.

Joanne remained quiet and withdrawn in those days following the divorce. She was there for her daughter in every possible way. But she cried at the drop of a hat. And the worst part of all was that she rarely worked on the book.

In the midst of this depression, she received a telephone call from her sister, who was now living in Edinburgh. Di suggested that Joanne might want to move to Edinburgh so that she could be near her family while she decided what she would do next. Joanne agreed, taking Jessica, her bags and the by now three chapters of *Harry Potter and the Philosopher's Stone*, and hopped on a train to Edinburgh. The journey was long and lonely. As the weather turned from bright sunshine to dark and foreboding, Joanne noted that it reflected her mood perfectly.

Although she was happy to be near her sister, once she arrived in Edinburgh, Joanne once again fell into deep despair. 'I had a tiny baby, no job, and I was in a strange place,' she painfully reflected in *People*.

These were not the best of times to be a single woman with a child in the UK. Just a month earlier, the British Prime Minister, John Major, had given a speech criticising single parents for being welfare-loving freeloaders. Joanne felt particularly offended by that speech. Yes, she was a single mother with a child. But she was also a college graduate with no shortage of skills. Certainly she would be able to keep her head above water.

But as she walked around Edinburgh with Jessica, Joanne often felt the hard stares of strangers. It was as if they knew.

A guardian angel named Sean appeared and loaned Joanne enough money to put a deposit down on what she once called 'a grotty flat'. With a roof over their heads, Joanne faced the dilemma of what to do. Her heart was set on finishing the *Harry Potter* book. But her dream was now complicated by the tiny bundle of joy asleep in her crib.

'I was terrified that I just wouldn't be able to justify to myself continuing to write,' she told *School Library Journal*. 'I thought it would benefit my daughter if I could earn a better living doing something else. If writing wasn't helping to buy new shoes, then it just felt very self-indulgent. What I was praying for was just to make enough for me to continue to write.'

Christmas was fast approaching and the festivities of the season only seemed to make Joanne feel worse. She had no money for presents for her daughter and the dear friends who had been there for her. Joanne felt coming to Edinburgh had been a hasty decision, so she made plans to return to London and attempt to find another job after the new year.

One rainy afternoon, as she was visiting her sister, Joanne, on an impulse, began telling her sister the story of Harry Potter, much as she had the story of Rabbit years before. Di was immediately caught by the

story and insisted that her older sister show
her what she had written.

'It's possible that if she had not laughed, I
would have set the whole thing to one side,'
recalled Joanne in the *Daily Telegraph*.

'But Di did laugh.'

6

DARK AND LIGHT

Making her sister laugh was the first positive experience Joanne had had in a long time. Encouraged that she might be on the right track with her book, Joanne made what she hoped would be a smart choice.

Joanne knew she would have no trouble finding another teaching job. But to do that would mean there would be no time left for writing. Finally she decided that she would finish the book in a year and try to get it published.

Joanne knew that this was a step that, once taken, could not be reversed. She was deliberately setting herself up for a hard time. But she also realised that she had spent years sitting on the fence about her writing, to no avail. To take a chance now would not put her in any worse a predicament then she was already in.

'I thought, What is the worst that could happen? Every publishing company in Britain could turn me down. Big deal,' she explained to the *Daily Telegraph*.

Thinking that gave the young mother strength. But she was not foolhardy in approaching this decision. Once she had made her mind up, 'my back was up against the wall, I knew I could not afford the luxury of writer's block'.

Any idea of working while she wrote went out of the window when she discovered that although she was eligible to receive financial aid, she was not eligible for childcare subsidy. Joanne was therefore forced into unemployment. The author would later recall that at that point she found herself in 'an appalling poverty trap' from which it seemed almost impossible to escape.

The whole process of applying for social support was humiliating and demoralising. Once again, she was getting those disapproving looks from strangers who saw her as something to be despised.

'That was probably the lowest point in my life,' she confessed to the *Boston Globe*. 'My self-respect was on the floor. I didn't want Jessica to grow up this way, so she became my inspiration and writing about Harry became my safe haven.'

Joanne soon discovered that many of her so-called friends were suddenly not there for her. They gave her strange looks and what conversations they had with her were strained and forced. But the young woman was also grateful for her sister and the handful of friends who stuck with her when the general attitude was that Joanne was nothing more than a freeloader. If she needed a few pounds to tide her over, they were there. But more important, on those days when the writing was not going well, Jessica was a handful, and she was feeling miserable, Joanne had people around who would just sit and listen as she poured her heart out.

Welfare support barely covered rent and food, so Joanne was forced to go to great lengths to save money. There were nights when there was barely enough food for mother and child, so Joanne would go to bed hungry. She could not even afford a used typewriter and, of course, even the most outdated computer was out of the question. So she would gather up scraps of paper and any pencils she could find and write out the adventures of Harry Potter in longhand.

Another problem was where to write. Her housing benefit only covered the rent on a cold, depressing one-room flat. This was hardly the place to inspire fantasy, and it was certainly not where Joanne wanted Jessica to spend the early part of her life. The struggling writer and mother put on her thinking cap and soon formulated an ingenious way to write and make her baby happy at the same time.

Every day she would put Jessica in her baby carrier and walk her around town until the child fell asleep. She would then head for one of a number of local cafés, where for the price of a cup of espresso and a glass of water, she could sit and write for a couple of hours while her daughter slept. Years later, Joanne would marvel at how much she had managed to write in those short periods of time.

One of her regular stops was the Nicolson Café, whose co-owner, Dougal McBride, remembered how he would glance up from his work and, sure enough, there would be Joanne writing away at a corner table.

'She was quite an odd sight,' he remembered in *People*. 'She would just push the pram with one hand and write away.'

Occasionally, Joanne would be too tired or the weather would be too bleak for her to risk taking Jessica out and about, so she would be forced to write in the flat. These were the times when Joanne would think that things could not get any worse.

However, through all the tough times, Joanne was buoyed up by the good cheer she was finding in writing her novel. As the pages continued to pile up, *Harry Potter* became her imaginary white knight, righting all the wrongs in her fantasy world that could not be fixed in her own. Her eyes would grow intense and her mouth would become fixed when she was devising the latest diabolical deed for Voldemort. And then there was wise old Dumbledore, whose every appearance in her manuscript was a time for inner joy and celebration.

'I wasn't really aware that it was a children's book,' she recalled in *Newsweek* of her feelings while writing *Harry Potter and the Philosopher's Stone*. 'I really wrote it for me. It was what I found funny and what I liked.'

As she had hoped, writing the *Harry Potter* fable was mentally and emotionally seeing her through the tough times. But as she neared the completion of the book, some of her old insecurities came flooding back. To fulfil her dream of becoming a writer, Joanne would have to risk all by sending the book out to publishers, who could dash her hopes without batting an eye.

Once she had decided that this was a risk worth taking, Joanne's next step was to decide just how one went about getting published. She had heard stories about how one needed an agent in order to be accepted by a book publisher. Now all she needed to do was find an agent.

Her first stop was the local library, where she found a writer's directory that listed the names and addresses of agents. Joanne pored over the directory and compiled a list of the agents she felt might be the most receptive to her book.

Harry Potter and the Philosopher's Stone was completed early in 1994. Joanne went over the manuscript carefully, rewriting and polishing until she finally had the book exactly as she had hoped. Because the cost of photocopying what had turned out to be an 80,000-word text was so prohibitive, Joanne, with the aid of a cheap typewriter she had managed to purchase, typed up two copies of her novel.

Then she sent the two copies to the top two agents on her list and hoped for the best.

1994 marked a turning point in Joanne's life. She had applied for and had received a grant from the Scottish Arts Council. The money was enough to allow Joanne to get proper childcare for Jessica during the day. Encouraged by this, she began looking for work and soon found a job in Edinburgh as a teacher of French at the Leith Academy and, later, at the Moray House Training College. True to her word, a year to the day that Joanne pulled into Edinburgh, penniless, she was now self-sufficient and off welfare benefits.

Joanne Rowling was feeling reborn.

In her spare time, Joanne continued to play around with *Harry Potter* and had soon come up with a storyline for a second book. She was hoping against hope that a second book would be possible. But thus far, there was nothing to convince her that it would ever come to pass.

'I had no idea truthfully what kind of reception it would get,' she explained in *School Library Journal*, 'if indeed it would ever get published, because I had never looked to publish before. I knew how difficult it would be and I was a completely unknown writer.'

One day, a letter arrived in the mail. Joanne could tell immediately it was from one of the agents to whom she had sent a copy of Harry. She was thrilled to get a response. But even as she tore open the envelope, 'I assumed it was a rejection note,' she recalled in the *Daily Telegraph*. 'But inside the envelope there was a letter saying "Thank you. We would be pleased to represent your manuscript on an exclusive basis." It was the best letter of my life. I read it eight times.'

Christopher Little was an all-business, no-frills type of person. But this unsolicited manuscript by a totally unknown writer had touched him. It was very well written, the story was entertaining and, like Joanne, he sensed that *Harry Potter and the Philosopher's Stone* was not entirely a children's book.

On meeting her, Christopher Little was also impressed with her enthusiasm and her struggle against formidable odds to get the book written. He also liked her grasp of reality. From his experience, Little knew that most children's authors struggle to make £2,000 a year and that they rarely end up becoming well known.

'When I went into this, my agent said to me, "I don't want you going away from this meeting thinking you're going to make a fortune,"' Joanne reported to *School Library Journal*. 'Then I said to him, "I know I'm not going to make any money out of it. I know I'm not going to be famous." All I ever wanted was for somebody to publish Harry so I could go to bookshops and see it.'

Christopher Little began sending out *Harry Potter and the Philosopher's Stone* to some of the biggest publishers in England. And as he had predicted, it was a long, hard road to publication. Before long, the first of a seemingly endless stream of rejections arrived at the agent's door. Some of the reasons given for not wanting to publish the book were that it was too long, too slow or too literary. Joanne was disappointed but was encouraged by Little's assessment that the book was too good not to be picked up at some point.

Joanne went about her business of being a mother and a teacher and tried to put the unenthusiastic reception to Harry out of her thoughts. But during the next year, she would often find herself day-dreaming about spying her book in the front window of the local bookshop. During those moments, she would find herself smiling at the events in her life that had brought her to this point.

In 1996, *Harry Potter and the Philosopher's Stone* finally found a home with British publisher Bloomsbury. Joanne was beside herself with joy when she heard the news. 'It was comparable only to having my daughter.'

True to Christopher Little's prediction, Bloomsbury offered the modest amount of £2,000.

'That was totally OK with me,' Joanne stated. 'All I wanted was to be able to support myself writing so I wouldn't have to give it up.'

As often happens in the publishing industry, word of mouth about the merit of the new book was good. Within months of Bloomsbury's purchase, inquiries from publishers all over the world began pouring in.

In 1997, the overwhelming interest in this children's book by an unknown writer had reached such a level that an auction was arranged at the time of the annual Bologna Book Fair held in Italy, at which foreign rights to books are sold. Joanne had been so thrilled at the prospect of Harry being published in her native England that she had paid only scant attention to what had been going on elsewhere in the world.

But she laughed when she recalled in *Salon* magazine the night her telephone rang at around 8.00pm. It was Christopher Little calling long-distance from New York.

'He said there was an auction taking place. An auction? I thought, Sotheby's, Christie's ...? Antiques? What is this all about? Then I realised that it was my book that was being auctioned off.'

At that very moment, thousands of miles away in a crowded room at the Bologna Book Fair, editorial director Arthur A Levine was about to take the biggest gamble of his life. The bidding on *Harry Potter and the Philosopher's Stone* had been in tense and the amounts being put up for the US rights had already reached astronomical levels. Levine, a spirited man with a ready smile, was about to make a bid that could change his life for ever.

'It's a scary thing when you keep bidding and the stakes are getting higher and higher,' said Levine in the *New York Times*. 'It's one thing to say I love this first novel by this unknown woman in Scotland and I want to publish it. It's another thing as the bidding goes higher. Do you love it this much? Do you love it at $50,000? At $70,000?'

The reason for Levine's concern was that the bidding was back to him and he was faced with the decision of offering an unheard-of bid of $100,000.

'I had never paid so much for an acquisition before. It was a great risk. If people believe in you and you flop, then you walk out on the plank and plunge.'

Little called Joanne again at 10.00pm that same evening. 'He said I should get ready because a Mr Levine of the *Scholastic Press* would pay a six-figure sum for the book and would be ringing me in a little bit. I nearly died.'

The tension mounted in Joanne's tiny Edinburgh flat. She was excited and scared all at the same time. She had hoped, under ideal circumstances, that a modest US sale would allow her to continue to write and teach on a part-time basis. But, she reasoned, things seemed to be moving much faster than anybody had expected.

The telephone rang promptly at 11.00pm. At the other end of the line, Levine was determined not to put any undue pressure on his new author. But his voice was shaking with excitement as he said hello.

'I called her very late,' he told the *New York Times*, 'and we had a very nice conversation. I said, "Don't be scared," and she said, "Thanks, I am." And we both said now that we've paid this much, we had to concentrate on making the book work.'

It was well past midnight when Joanne, after checking on her sleeping daughter, finally went to bed.

'But I couldn't sleep. On one level, I was obviously delighted,' she told a *Salon* magazine reporter. 'But most of me was just frozen in terror.'

7

HARRY CONQUERS THE WORLD

*J*oanne had good reason to be fearful in the weeks following her big signing with Scholastic Books.

The amount of money involved was so unheard of in children's book circles that the book publishing gossip was that Arthur Levine and Scholastic had taken leave of their senses. Many pessimists predicted that no matter how good the book was, it would certainly not make anywhere near enough to earn back the massive advance.

Joanne's agent and Arthur Levine assured her that Scholastic Books was not in the habit of laying out huge amounts of money for books they felt would fail. Joanne was not completely convinced. But that was only part of her concern.

Word of this author who had landed an unprecedented advance for a children's book had quickly spread around the world. The normally shy woman was now being deluged with requests for interviews and her picture was appearing in newspapers and magazines. And this was before her book was even published in Great Britain.

If it had been up to her, Joanne would have done no publicity for the book at all. But she felt a strong sense of loyalty to those who had taken this chance with her, so she agreed to every request.

'The stakes had seemed to have gone up a lot,' she told an interviewer in 1999. 'I attracted a lot of publicity for which I was totally unprepared.'

Joanne was not big on change, and the idea of doing interviews in stuffy hotel rooms and television studios ran contrary to her nature. So when she started entertaining the press, she would gently insist that, whenever possible, interviews be done at her familiar table in the Nicholson Café.

When these interviews took place, a crowd of waiters and waitresses would stand on the periphery listening. They would smile as Joanne explained how she would sit at this very table and write under the most trying of conditions. Many of them had served her when she was down on her luck. Now they were as proud as they could possibly be that their regular customer was a well-known author.

Initially, she was not comfortable doing interviews. Joanne was not always fluent in her responses and worried about the kind of impression she was making. But she knew only how to be honest, and the press were going to make of that what they would.

Much of that early publicity put Joanne on the defensive. In many newspaper and magazine interviews, the reporters painted a picture of Joanne as a penniless, divorced single mother living on welfare and writing at her leisure in cafés. She had no problem with the accuracy and, yes, it was true. But she felt 'knocked sideways' by the negative image it presented of her and the fact that it was forcing her to relive what she considered one of the saddest periods of her life.

Joanne was quick to clarify that she had been gainfully employed since 1990, when she started writing Harry, and that the only reason she had to go on welfare was that the system in Edinburgh would not allow for childcare. And then, she insisted, it was only for the year that she was completing the book.

As *Harry Potter and the Philosopher's Stone* was going through the publishing process in England, Joanne found that there was one more compromise she was being asked to make. The publishers, fearful that a book with a woman's name on the cover might not attract young boys, asked if Joanne would mind if she were listed as JK Rowling. Joanne thought it was an odd request but saw no harm in going along with the notion.

Harry Potter and the Philosopher's Stone was published in England in 1997. The book was an immediate smash hit, selling more than 150,000 copies in a matter of months. Reviewers fell over themselves in praise of the book.

One critic stated, 'The book is an unassailable stand for the power of fresh, innovative storytelling.' Another commented, 'Rowling's ability to put a fantastic spin on sports, student rivalry and eccentric faculty contributes to the humour, charm and delight of her utterly captivating story.'

By the end of the year, JK Rowling's first novel had garnered up a number of prestigious awards, including the Nestlé Smarties Book Prize, the Federation of Children's Books Group Award and the British Book Awards Children's Book of the Year. A little into 1998, the book had sold a total of half a million copies, an unprecedented number for a children's book.

Joanne was thrilled and more than a bit amused at what was happening with Harry. She was hard-pressed to answer the question she often asked as a child. Why?

'I suppose it's mainly word of mouth,' she suggested in response to the book's success in the *Guardian*. 'I think children just tell one another about it.'

But she did have a good laugh at the notion that the reason so many books were being sold was because a good many of them were being snapped up by adults just as eager to read the adventures of Harry as their children. As an example, she cited a story she had heard from a friend who had seen a man in a suit on a train reading a copy behind his newspaper.

'I had not aimed the books at children,' she once said. 'I only wrote them for me.'

With the money from her US book deal and another eight countries rolling in, Joanne was slowly beginning to adjust to the idea of not being poor. But it did not come in one handy lump sum. She agonised for a long time whether to purchase a £75 coat so that she would look smart for her television appearances.

But with the success of *Harry Potter and the Philosopher's Stone* in England and the American edition due out shortly, Joanne decided it was time to leave poverty behind her. The first thing she did was rent a house in Edinburgh. Nothing fancy, just well-lit rooms, heating and comfortable furniture. However, for Joanne, it was pure heaven and relief.

'I no longer have the constant worry of whether Jessica will outgrow a pair of shoes before I've got the money for the next pair,' she said in a *Daily Telegraph* article.

Joanne was already hard at work on the follow-up to *Harry Potter and the Philosopher's Stone* before it had been published. So when she was not handling the increasing demand for interviews or tending to her daughter, Joanne was churning out pages of what would ultimately be titled *Harry Potter and the Chamber of Secrets*. But while she was now able to afford a computer and Jessica was of an age where she was spending part of the day in pre-school, little of Joanne's approach to writing had changed.

Every day, after kissing her daughter goodbye, Joanne would walk down to Nicholson's Café, pull up a chair at a table next to an upstairs window, pull out paper and a pen, and begin writing. The first time she did this after her first book had been accepted, the waiter, who had served her regularly when she was down and out, did a double take when she asked for a menu. One reason for continuing the routine was that Joanne felt lonely at the prospect of sitting in her house, by herself, in front of a computer.

'Writing and cafés are strongly linked in my brain,' she recently revealed to the press. 'I still write in longhand. I like physically shuffling around with papers.'

Harry Potter and the Chamber of Secrets was almost complete and ready for publication when the US edition of *Harry Potter and the Philosopher's Stone* was available in August 1998. The British mania for *Harry Potter* was soon duplicated in the USA as children and adults fell in love with Harry and his adventures.

Soon, editions of Joanne's first book were published in nearly 30 other countries. Joanne would have a giggle at the different languages and, in some cases, the different cover designs which bound the books. As each new edition was released, her happiness increased.

Publishers on both sides of the Atlantic were now convinced that *Harry Potter* was no fluke, so contracts were quickly drawn up that would have Joanne writing a total of seven *Harry Potter* books in the coming years. Joanne was thrilled. Then she was scared to death.

In a practical sense, the longevity of the contract meant she would never want for anything for her daughter or herself. But there were also what she described as 'a few weeks of terror' as she contemplated whether she could write the remainder of the books with the same enthusiasm now that the whole world was looking over her shoulder.

To relieve the fear of writer's block, Joanne sat down and plotted out the remaining five *Harry Potter* books. She was painstaking in figuring out the storylines, the specific elements of each adventure, and the important message that readers young and old would take away from each book. At the end of this plotting session, Joanne emerged confident in her ability to finish Harry Potter's education.

'And I finally realised what the most important thing for me was,' she stated in the *Boston Globe*. 'I love writing these books. I don't think anyone could enjoy reading them more than I enjoy writing them.'

Harry Potter and the Chamber of Secrets was published in July 1998 and, like its predecessor, was an immediate blockbuster all over the world. In the UK alone, the book outsold the latest novels by bestselling writers such as John Grisham and Tom Clancy.

Joanne continued to be amazed at the way people had taken Harry Potter and his world to their hearts and minds. But the writer was also finding that those bestselling books were also beginning to complicate her life. Already well into writing her third book, *Harry Potter and the Prisoner of Azkaban*, Joanne was finding that she had less time to write because of interviews, book signings and various lectures and school appearances.

Joanne was a good sport when it came to things like that. In the case of the book signings and appearances at schools, she loved the idea of actually meeting with the children who were reading her books.

'As an ex-teacher, it's just so liberating to go in front of a class simply to entertain them and it's great when they've read the books and can quote you passages and know the characters,' she said in the *Guardian*.

But there were also those days when things did not go according to plan and Joanne found herself overwhelmed to the point of tears. During what seemed like an endless round of promotional duties surrounding the release of *Harry Potter and the Chamber of Secrets*, Joanne was having trouble checking out of a London hotel. At first, the hotel would not allow her to check out because there was no record of her name in the computer. Finally, a hotel manager found her name but insisted that she could not leave until she had paid her bill. This upset the normally unflappable Joanne because she knew that her publisher had already sorted it out. With the hotel confusion finally straightened out, she hopped into a taxi, now quite late for an interview. Half-way there, Joanne realised that she had left the hotel without her purse.

It was all too much. Joanne burst into tears, startling the taxi driver.

However, generally, her good humour and sunny outlook carried Joanne through the difficulty of being in the public eye. She felt incredibly fortunate to be in this position because it had come as a result of her unwillingness to give up on her dream. So, yes, she would give interviews and talk to people about Harry until the cows came home.

But at the end of the day, she would happily race home to comfort Jessica. As she held her young daughter and asked about her day at school, Joanne was proud – proud that as her mother, she was able to provide Jessica with security and a good life.

And if there was time, Joanne would walk down to Nicholson's Café, where she might find a few moments to write. She would sometimes order the usual espresso and water. But, just as often, she would also pick up the menu, and without worrying about the price, choose something to eat.

8

HARRY EVER AFTER

*H*arry Potter and the Prisoner of Azkaban was published late in 1998. The mania for Harry continued as the book immediately followed its predecessors to the top of the world's bestseller lists.

Reporters once again came around, hoping the quiet author of these fantastic adventures would be able to supply the background to Harry Potter's continued success. And, once again, Joanne found it hard to come up with an answer that did not have the words 'shocked and amazed' somewhere in it.

Happily, Joanne was more than willing to try.

'I am still stunned that I went from being an unknown writer on the breadline to having my books at the top of the charts. It's truly amazing,' she would regularly tell reporters.

But not all the news was good. A number of religious groups had decided that the *Harry Potter* books were endorsing evil themes and attitudes. Many of these groups sent letters to newspapers objecting to the books and, in some cases, they tried to have the books banned from libraries and bookstores.

Joanne was upset by their actions but chose to ignore them. Eventually, the storm of protest passed.

Joanne celebrated New Year's Eve 1999 quietly with a small group of friends. At the stroke of midnight, she toasted her good fortune and her good friends. She could only imagine what the forthcoming year would offer.

A resolution was not long in coming. Nobody had ever referred to Joanne as a workaholic. But as fast as the new Harry books were coming out, one had to wonder if Joanne did anything but write. She repeatedly stated that writing was the thing she most liked to do. However, she did decide that she owed it to herself and Jessica to get away every once in a while. So she began travelling, taking short jaunts to neighbouring countries that would allow Jessica and her to explore pastures new and escape the distractions that were always a phone call away in Edinburgh.

It came as no surprise that Hollywood was soon wild about Harry as well. Movie-makers immediately saw the possibilities of *Harry Potter* as a movie. No fewer than a dozen film studios were actively pursuing the rights to turn *Harry Potter* into a full-length motion picture. Once again, Joanne was glued to the telephone as Christopher Little relayed the latest messages regarding a film contract. But the negotiation of film deals, unlike that of book deals, tend to drag on for ages, so Joanne was content to continue with the business of writing the fourth instalment of *Harry Potter*.

With two books out in the same year, Joanne was given more time to devise Harry's latest adventure. There had been some concern from the publisher that writing two books literally back to back might have put a bit of a strain on their favourite author. However, Joanne was nothing if not anxious, after the seemingly endless round of press and publicity, to get back to creating another exciting *Harry Potter* adventure for her legion of fans.

The routine remained pretty much the same. Although her notoriety had made the Nicholson Café a sudden tourist attraction, and Joanne would occasionally find herself feeling self-conscious at being gawped at by people who had come to watch her work, she would still find time to sit and work there a few hours almost every day. But, out of necessity, she was also working in other cafés and pubs, which she wisely refused to name.

Wherever she went, the writing continued to go smoothly. The characters had become like a second family to her. She knew what would work and what would appear false. Creating new names for her outlandish characters was always a joy. But Joanne had to admit that with this book, things were beginning to change. Harry and the other characters were now well into their teenage years. She felt it was time to have Harry discover girls.

This was an exciting turn of events for Joanne, one that allowed her to revisit her own adolescence as a blueprint for how Harry should react the first time he sees a girl as something other than a good buddy. Harry was never boring, but now there was an extra element of excitement that would have Joanne snatching up her pen and paper at every opportunity.

Shortly before the turn of the New Year 2000, Joanne, with Jessica by her side, boarded a plane at London's Heathrow Airport and headed for the USA on a three-week book tour. These were exciting times for Joanne. She had heard about how well the first three books had done in America, but she was anxious to meet with her readers face to face and experience the joy and excitement they had for her work with her own eyes.

At each and every stop on this cross-country tour, Joanne was very much the teacher in her dealings with the thousands of fans who lined up to see her. She would encourage them to read and write as often as possible. She would chuckle at the inevitable question on how to pronounce her name before saying, 'It's Roe-ling, not Row-ling.' The woman of simple tastes grew to like the rock-star treatment she was receiving with limo rides and high security at every stop. The look on Joanne's face was worth a thousand words. But only one was really necessary – joy.

The year 2000 would bring continued success for Joanne. *Harry Potter and the Goblet of Fire* was ready for an 8 July publication date. It was also announced during this period that Warner Brothers had secured the rights to make the movie version of *Harry Potter and the Philosopher's Stone*. Originally, the studio had stated that Steven Spielberg was interested in directing the film. But the director would later bow out of the project, saying, 'My directorial interests were taking me in another direction.' Eventually, the studio made its choice and assigned a talented director,

Chris Columbus, and a screenwriter, Steven Kloves, to adapt Joanne's fantasy world to the screen.

Joanne agreed to Warner Brothers' offer on the condition that she would have input into the screenplay and that the movie would be live action rather than animation. But as the studio officially announced that *Harry Potter* would be in cinemas by in the summer of 2001, she had to admit to being nervous about the prospect of seeing Harry on the big screen.

'It's actually a mixture of excitement and nervousness,' she said upon hearing the good news. 'I do think Harry would make a great film. But obviously I do feel protective toward the characters I've lived for with so long.'

In March, director Columbus flew to Scotland, where he and Joanne met. Both came away from the meeting enthusiastic about the film.

'I'm terribly excited,' said Columbus in the *Los Angeles Times*. 'My oldest daughter, Eleanor, who is ten, got me into the books over a year ago. Between my four kids and their friends, I've heard a lot about what this movie should be and how I could ruin it if I cut this or that scene. I won't let anyone down. It will be a faithful adaptation.'

Joanne was also in good spirits about her sudden involvement in the movie business.

'I'm more involved than I thought I would be. I can't wait to see how they will pull off a Quidditch game.'

The publicity campaign for the release of *Harry Potter and the Goblet of Fire* reached massive proportions as the days counted down to the official publication date. At this point, Joanne was not looking forward to answering the same questions over and over again; she had in recent months started saying 'No' to all but the most important publicity events just so she would have time to write.

Her publishers took the hint and, in late spring, announced that Joanne would do one 90-minute interview session in London and that would be it. Soon, journalists from all over the world were flying in for the opportunity to ask the world's most popular author questions about her new book and her life in general.

Joanne was a bit nervous at the prospect of facing so many reporters at the same time and was concerned that this massive press conference would get out of control. But much of the questioning turned out to be highly predictable. There were the usual questions about why Harry had proven to be so popular, Joanne's struggles in Edinburgh, and how she was coping with success. Joanne fielded them with ease and responded with good humour and concisely. But there were some surprise announcements along the way.

Joanne revealed that an important character would die in the fourth book and that Harry would develop his first crush on a girl. The author also hinted that, in the fifth book, readers would finally discover why Harry continues to spend his summers with the frightful Dursleys.

The secretive author also stated that Harry's parents would not return and that she had decided long ago that magic could not bring back the dead. But she did hint that Harry's parents would continue to be an important part of future books.

Joanne left the press conference relieved that the most difficult aspect of the whole exercise was once again behind her. Now she could get back to the fun part – the writing itself.

Joanne continued to feel anxious as 8 July got closer and closer. At this point, nobody was betting against the fact that *Harry Potter and the Goblet of Fire* would do as well, if not better, than her previous three books. But Joanne was never one to take anything for granted.

Finally, the date arrived and Joanne crossed her fingers as her latest *Harry Potter* adventure went on sale in the UK and the USA at the same time. Within hours, the first reports began to come in. Bookstores were selling out of copies in a matter of minutes and were already on the telephone to re-order. Within days, the book was high up on the bestseller charts around the world. Joanne heaved a sigh of relief at the news.

The magic of *Harry Potter* was as strong as ever.

Joanne saw the summer of 2000 come and go in a state of undisguised happiness. She was already hard at work on the next *Harry* instalment. She was happy and healthy, and she had a wonderful daughter to boot.

But with the beginning of book number five, the end was now in sight. Harry Potter would graduate from his seven years of schooling at Hogwarts.

And although she would occasionally tease the public about 'never say never' when asked if she would follow Harry off to college, the author has remained adamant that Harry Potter will end with book number seven.

She has admitted to feeling sad at the idea that Harry's adventures will end one day and feels that there will be a 'bereavement' when she has written the last line on the final page. But she insists that 'there will be no Harry Potter midlife crisis or Harry Potter as an old wizard'.

But as she nears the end of the year 2000, Joanne could not be happier. Her career has exceeded all her expectations. She has a beautiful daughter and she is making a living doing what she loves to do. And she is not sad at the fact that there is no man in her life. Her feeling on that topic is that if Mr Perfect were to come along, she would be thrilled.

'But it's not my top priority,' she told

Salon magazine. 'Right now my life is very fulfilled.'

While her future after *Harry Potter* is still up in the air, the author knows that writing will be at the centre of it. It is all she knows, and she feels putting pen to paper is necessary for her. Joanne once admitted that 'I don't feel normal when I haven't written for a while.'

Joanne has hinted many times that her next step after Harry would be to write more adult novels. But she is honest enough to accept that she will probably never write anything as popular as Harry, and that is all right with her.

'I will have lived with Harry for 13 years and I know I'll probably have to take some time off to grieve. But then I'll be on with the next book.'

What that will be is anybody's guess, including Joanne's. But she knows where she will go for inspiration. 'I might just get on another train.'

9

TOUCHED BY AN ANGEL

*T*wo dramas were unfolding in July 1999. In her home in Edinburgh, Scotland, Joanne was working day and night in an attempt to finish *Harry Potter and the Goblet of Fire*. She was refusing all interview requests and avoiding any distractions that would keep her from finishing the long anticipated fourth adventure of Harry Potter. The fame and celebrity status that had grown up around

Joanne had caused her to alter her writing routine. Her phone rang constantly, interrupting her quiet time in the room in her house that doubled as her office and writing room. And though she continued to spend much of each day writing at the table of her favourite outdoor restaurant, Nicholson's, word had gotten out and she was often interrupted by sightseers requesting a photo or an autograph. Eventually she began writing in other restaurants around town in an attempt to find the time to finally finish *Goblet of Fire*. Joanne was finding that dealing with fame was not always easy.

At the same time, in Toronto, Canada, nine-year-old Natalie McDonald was dying of leukemia.

Natalie was the ultimate Harry Potter fan. She lived and breathed Joanne's stories from the beginning, and it was Harry Potter's flights of fantasy that had helped the young girl cope with her pain and her illness. A family friend, Annie Kidder, wanted to do something special to make Natalie's last days a bit more pleasant and felt that hearing from her favourite author would make the young girl deliriously happy.

Annie found the address of Joanne's London publisher and sent a series of letters, emails and faxes, explaining Natalie's dire situation and requesting some kind of response from the author. The people in the publishing office were touched by the sincerity of Annie's messages and, despite Joanne's strict order not to be disturbed as she raced to complete *Harry Potter and the Goblet of Fire*, they believed this heartfelt request was something she would respond to. Finally the latest letter from Annie Kidder was forwarded to Joanne's Edinburgh home.

Joanne was not there to receive it.

After an intense period of writing, Joanne felt she needed a break and so had decided, in mid July, to take a short vacation in Spain. Annie's letter had arrived the day after Joanne left. When she returned from her holiday, the first thing she read was the letter from Annie. She was touched and saddened by her young fan's illness and immediately felt compelled to do something to help.

'But I had a bad feeling that I was too late,' she told Maclean's.

Joanne called Annie Kidder but she was not at home. She instantly dashed off a long letter and emailed a copy to Natalie and her mother, Valerie. The email arrived on August 4, 1999.

Sadly, Joanne would later discover that her message had arrived too late. Natalie had died on August 3.

But Annie would recall Joanne's kind words in that letter. She treated the dying young girl with respect and lovingly talked about her books and characters. In the body of that letter, Joanne also revealed the story and secrets of *Harry Potter and the Goblet of Fire*, a full eleven months before the book was to be released.

This might have been the end of a very sad story.

But Joanne had other ideas. The author, heartbroken by her inability to bring comfort to the young child's final days, had been so moved by Natalie and her life struggles and devotion to Harry Potter that she decided to honour the girl she had never met by writing her into a passage of *Harry Potter and the Goblet of Fire*. And so on page 159 of *Goblet of Fire*, Joanne created a scene in which the sorting hat sends first year student Natalie McDonald to Harry's Gryffindor house. This would be the only time Joanne would ever use a real person's name in a Harry Potter book.

After receiving Joanne's letter to her daughter, Natalie's mother, Valerie, wrote back on behalf of her daughter to thank the author for her efforts. Joanne was touched by Valerie's letter and a regular correspondence began between the two women. As the letters went back and forth between Canada and Scotland, Joanne found that she had discovered, in Valerie, a kindred spirit, someone, who like Joanne, had experienced the death of a loved one, and who felt strongly about the importance and challenges of motherhood.

As the time for publication of *Harry Potter and the Goblet of Fire* neared, Joanne and Valerie agreed to meet in England to cement their relationship face to face. And so, in July 2000, Valerie, her husband and two other daughters travelled to England to meet with Joanne.

Joanne was unsure how this meeting would go. She had always been a very private person and this kind of friendship was out of character for her. But the kindness and love expressed in their letters had found a special place in Joanne's heart and so she felt comfortable about meeting this woman.

The meeting between the two women was a joyous, bittersweet time. There were hugs all round, tears of joy and happiness were shed in the memory of a child whom Valerie had lost and Joanne had never known but, in a very spiritual sense, had come to know.

It was during their London visit that Valerie and her family, on a sightseeing excursion around the city on the London tube, discovered Joanne's secret memorial to Natalie. To pass the time on the tube, Valerie began reading *Harry Potter and the Goblet of Fire* to her daughters. One can only imagine the surprise when she turned to page 159 and discovered how Joanne had chosen to honour the memory of Natalie.

Natalie McDonald was in heaven. But in the heart and mind of Joanne Kathleen Rowling, she would forever live in Hogwarts.

10

THE HOGWARTS EXPRESS

A light blue car pulled to a stop at London's King's Cross Station on July 8, 2000. Inside, Joanne was still rubbing the sleep from her eyes at the early morning wakeup. She was already missing her daughter, Jessica, who would be sleeping soundly in the home of her sister, Di, as she prepared to catch a train.

Looking outside, Joanne saw a scene of total chaos. A literal army of photographers and reporters had lined the railway station entrance, television cameras jockeying for a good position, people being pushed and shoved every which way. Beyond the cluster of press people and behind a barricade stood more than three hundred children and their bewildered parents, who had braved the cold weather and the early hour for the chance to see their favourite author.

Sadly, while the photographers and reporters were given free rein to move wherever they wanted, the children were being kept in that one spot, making even a glimpse of Joanne all but impossible.

As she emerged from the car, a fresh-off-the-press copy of *Harry Potter and the Goblet of Fire* clutched in her hands, a shout went up from a group of photographers who begged: 'Give us a wave, Jo!' For Joanne, it was a bit early in the morning for this sort of thing. But after a moment's hesitation, she rolled her eyes, presented a half smile, half grimace to the photographers, and offered up a half hearted wave as the flashbulbs exploded around her like lightning.

'It's rather mad isn't it?' she joked with photographers as they snapped away. 'I'd really like to talk with some children if I ever manage to finish with you lot.'

With that, Joanne made a break through the crowd and instinctively made for the children. Sadly, she was intercepted by public relations people and ushered back toward the waiting cameras.

'I'm sorry,' she yelled at the children as she was hustled away. 'I'm not allowed.'

Surrounded by personal assistants and representatives of her British publishing company, Joanne made her way through the station and to Platform 9 ¾ where she came face to face with The Queen of Scots which, for the occasion, made over into a real life incarnation of The Hogwarts Express. The train, an old fashioned, red, steam-powered engine, not unlike the fictional train that takes Harry Potter to the

School of Witchcraft and Wizardry, is pouring smoke out of its towering stack. Behind it, an observation car and a sleeping car are rapidly filling up with people. Joanne stops in front of the train and smiles gamely one last time for the photographers and steps aboard.

The Hogwarts Express will be Joanne's home for the next four days.

As part of a massive publicity stunt to kick off the official publication of *Harry Potter and the Goblet of Fire*, Joanne agreed to go on a train tour, beginning at London's King's Cross station and ending at Perth, Scotland. The train would make stops at train stations along the way and Joanne would sign books for a limited number of children, whose names were chosen in drawings sponsored by bookstores at bookstores, museums or the train stations at each stop. It was a grand idea to help promote her new book, but Joanne saw the train ride as something much more important ... an opportunity to meet her young readers face to face.

'I love reading to child readers,' she said in Maclean's. 'They ask the best questions. The children talk about the characters as though they're mutual friends I happen to know a bit better.'

Promptly at 11.27 am, the train began to slowly pull out of the station amid the crush of television cameras, news reporters and the number of children who had awakened as early as 4 am just so they could get to the station and see their favorite author off. Joanne sensed her young fan's disappointment and stuck her head out the window and waved at the children.

'Oh God. I'm sorry. I'm sorry,' she called out to the children. 'It was nice meeting you all.'

Joanne was saddened at what she considered to be the shabby treatment of her young fans, and at the same time more than a little overwhelmed by the enormous interest in her latest book. She vowed to make it up to the children at the first opportunity. As for all the cameras going off and the reporters treating every word that tumbled out of her mouth as gold – she did not know if she would ever get used to it.

Joanne took a quick tour of the train. She immediately fell in love with the dining car, whose plush brocade furnishings seemed fit for royalty and would offer her a wonderful view of the countryside as the train flew past. The dining car was decked out in antique elegance, a finery reserved for the kings and queens these cars had once carried. And, at the end of the day, the sleeping car would assuredly provide her with pleasant dreams.

Amid darkening clouds and the promise of a summer rain, the train left King's Cross and pulled steadily out of London, the train cars beginning to rock and rattle, as they would for the remainder of the trip. Not long after leaving King's Cross, the steam engine unceremoniously broke down and a modern day diesel was recruited to tow the older train for the remainder of the trip.

Inside, Joanne had made herself comfortable and was beginning the first of many interviews with the members of the press on board. It was a time of reflection as, once again, she told the story of how Harry Potter came to be, the latest news regarding the Harry Potter movie and the behind the scenes stories of writing *Harry Potter and the Goblet of Fire*. And there were many new revelations. For the first time, Joanne candidly revealed that she had, in fact, been late completing the book, due in part to having scrapped the manuscript and started over when she realized that her presentation of the story and the characters was not consistent with the three previous books and would not reach the conclusion she wanted. And, for the first time of many, she tried to express her reaction to the continued worldwide popularity of the Harry Potter books.

'I can't explain it,' she offered a reporter from the *New York Times* at one point. 'I don't have an answer. I just write what I wanted to write. I write what amuses me. It's totally for myself. I never in my wildest dreams expected this popularity.'

The first stop for The Hogwarts Express was a mid-afternoon signing at Didicot Railway Centre in the town of Didicot. That first night the train chugged into the Kidderminster Station in the Severen Valley. Joanne appreciated the logistics of the tour. The plan included big and small cities alike, and the trip was reminding Joanne of the old days when she travelled everywhere by train.

On the second day of the tour, the fantasy train stopped in the cities of Manchester and York. By the third day, the train had left Newcastle and had crossed over into Scotland and into her hometown of Edinburgh, where Joanne was greeted as a hometown hero.

It was the same at every stop. The train would pull into the station and Joanne would be whisked away to a local bookstore, where she would meet a selected group of her fans and sign their books. More often than not though, she would meet and greet her admirers at the train station.

As always, Joanne would put on her best smiling face despite the frequent early morning stops on the schedule and the fact she readily had admitted in Readers Digest that 'I'm really not a morning person'. But nothing, including the fact that she was already missing Jessica, would stop her from being the embodiment of all her fan's fantasies ... even if only for a moment.

There were wondrous stories of the lengths that many of her fans went to to get an audience with Joanne. A twelve-year-old boy won a coveted ticket to meet Joanne by winning a complex Harry Potter trivia quiz. Upon hearing that a London bookstore was giving away tickets, one persistent girl awoke at 4 am and was in line outside the bookstore at 6.30 am, hours before the store was due to open. Still another young girl had sadly thought that she had lost out on the drawing but was miraculously rewarded with a ticket when one of the original winners gave up his ticket to attend an athletic event.

And at each stop along the tour, the reaction from the children was always the same ... shock, delight, amazement and a sudden inability to speak. To finally get to meet the creator of their fantasies was, according to a description of the scene by an *Entertainment Weekly* reporter, 'deliriously mind boggling'.

The excitement generated by Joanne's appearances was best summed up by one ten year old who emerged from a brief meeting with Joanne and exclaimed, 'Am I allowed to faint now?'

Finally, on the fourth day, The Hogwarts Express pulled into the railroad station at

Perth, Scotland. Joanne was both relieved and excited that this was the last stop on her book tour. She greeted this last group of anxious fans with a broad smile and a respectful attitude. As she signed this last batch of books, she was able to ask each child about what they liked about the books and who their favourite character was. At one point, a child was asked to pose with Joanne for a photograph. The child appeared to be nervous at being pushed into the spotlight, but Joanne calmed him when she jokingly said, 'Pretend that you're thrilled to see me.'

Finally, with the last book signed, Joanne got into a car for a one-hour ride back to her house in Edinburgh. During the ride back, she looked out the window at the passing scenery and reflected on the turn her life had taken. In the past year, she had been named by the prestigious *Forbes Magazine* as one of the top 25 most powerful celebrities in the world. In June 2000, she had made a quick trip to Dartmouth College in New

Hampshire where she received her first honorary degree. But easily the high point for Joanne came in the past month when she was summoned to Buckingham Palace, where she was awarded The Order Of The British Empire by the Royal Family.

There were other more personal memories to relive. There was the joy in watching Jessica grow into quite the wonderful young girl, turning six and entering school. Because she did not feel Jessica had been old enough to comprehend the world of Harry Potter, Joanne had decided that she would not begin to read the stories to her until her daughter turned seven. But what she discovered is that the children in her daughter's class were already quite familiar with her work and so they were constantly coming up to Jessica asking her questions about Harry that she did not have the answers to.

'She didn't have any idea what they were all talking about,' Joanne once explained to

Entertainment Weekly. 'And I just thought, I'm excluding her from this huge part of my life, and it's making her an outsider. So I read them to her and she became completely Harry Potter obsessed.'

And there were the obvious changes that had taken place in her own life as the result of the worldwide popularity of Harry Potter. She had more money than she ever dreamed of having. But she spent wisely, ensuring a wonderful life for herself and Jessica. But the added attention was not always welcome. Before her Harry Potter books became a global sensation, Joanne was still able to move about Edinburgh without being recognized and could still spend hours writing at her favorite cafe, while listening to good music and sipping from a seemingly bottomless cup of coffee.

But with the publication of the third Harry Potter book, *Harry Potter and the Prisoner of Azkaban*, Joanne began to notice an increasing lack of privacy. With her writing habits now well publicised, she soon became the centre of attention as she would write at an outside table of a café. And although people were always pleasant when approaching her, it would often conflict with what she insisted on being her ideal writing day.

'In an ideal day, I'll work six to ten hours,' she told a Knight Ridder News Service reporter. 'But now I'm fighting to get the time to write. I use cafes like offices and I try to get away from the house whenever possible.'

But with her notoriety, Joanne had found herself spending more and more time writing at home. And even that did not protect her from regular interruptions.

'There was a phase when I had journalists at my front door quite a lot,' she related to a *Newsweek* reporter. 'And that was quite horrible. That was not something I had ever anticipated happening to me, and it's not pleasant.'

But, like every other element of her newfound celebrity, Joanne had learned to deal with it. Which is why she took things like this just concluded publicity trip in support of *Harry Potter and the Goblet of Fire* in her stride. The town of Edinburgh was rounding into view. Joanne saw the familiar streets and buildings. In a short time, she would be taking Jessica in her arms and holding her tight.

Joanne Kathleen Rowling was the most famous author on the planet. But tonight she would just be Mum.

For the next couple of months, Joanne would once again return to normal pursuits. Every morning she would walk Jessica to school and pick her up at the end of the day. And she would find time to do some window shopping along Edinburgh's Princess Street. She also did more interviews, a handful of appearances in bookstores in and around London and, to spare Jessica somewhat from the constant

questions of classmates, Joanne did a pair of lectures as a reward for the two top performing classes in her daughter's school.

Joanne also began to turn her attention to charitable causes. She agreed to become the spokeswoman for the National Council for One Parent Families and donated £500,000 to the charity, whose emphasis was on helping single mothers. This was obviously a cause that was near and dear to Joanne's heart.

'I had a degree, a profession, and friends who were willing to lend me money when I badly needed it,' she said in a speech before the organization. 'So if I met obstacles pulling myself out of the benefits system, how much more difficult must it be for people who don't have the same advantages? Seven years after becoming a lone parent, I feel qualified to look anyone I meet in the eye and say that people bringing up children single handedly deserve not condemnation, but congratulation.'

Joanne's charitable outlook also led to her establishing the Harry Potter Fund with the charity group Comic Relief UK, an organisation dedicated to helping children in the UK and Africa.

Finally, when she had a few moments to herself, she secretly began writing the fifth Harry Potter book, *Harry Potter and the Order of the Phoenix*.

'I literally don't feel quite right if I haven't written for a while,' she confessed during a *Newsweek* interview. 'A week is about as long as I can go without getting extremely edgy. It really is a compulsion.'

As summer began to turn to autumn, Joanne realized that the quiet times were about to end and that she would soon be giving a reading before the largest audience she could ever imagine. The odyssey that would take her to Canada had begun almost a year earlier when she was racing to complete *Harry Potter and the Goblet of Fire*.

'I was feeling very fraught at the time,' she

told a Canadian Broadcast Corporation interviewer. 'I was halfway through book four and I said yes. At that point, I did say yes to quite a lot of things just to stop people from asking me anything else because I really wanted to be writing. Then I sort of emerged from the madness that had been book four.'

And realized exactly what she had said yes to.

As part of the festivities of the Vancouver International Writers' Festival, Joanne had agreed to do a pair of readings in the famed Pacific Coliseum in front of a projected sold out audience of six thousand. But when word had leaked out that Joanne would be attending, the demand for tickets was so great that the festival directors had come back to Joanne with the request that she give an additional reading the day before in the Toronto Sky Dome, the home of the Toronto Blue Jays baseball team, in front of a projected 20,000 young fans.

'I realized how big the reading was going to be and then I got terrified,' she told the CBC interviewer.

Once she got over her initial fears, Joanne was thrilled at the prospect of going to Canada for the first time. The writer had always had a warm feeling about the country and its people and was looking forward to experiencing both at first hand in what would be a six-day visit.

Joanne first flew to New York City, where she spent a couple of days meeting with her American publisher and giving a handful of magazine and newspaper interviews. Some of the questions covered familiar ground, but a few odd things had popped up in the wake of the publication of *Harry Potter and the Goblet of Fire* that she needed to address. One of the most outrageous to Joanne's many readers was the fact that, in the final sequence of the fourth book, there was a mistake in the order that Harry's parents emerge from Voldemort's wand. In the previous three books, Joanne had said on several occasions that Voldemort had killed James first and Lily second. But in *Goblet of Fire* we are told that the ghosts would emerge in reverse order – James steps out of the wand before Lily. Joanne exclaimed that it was just an unfortunate editing error that would be corrected in later editions of the book.

She was also questioned about why she was two months late in handing in the final manuscript of *Harry Potter and the Goblet of Fire*. She conceded that the book had been the hardest one to write and, while she had always taken great pains to be consistent in her story elements, that the plot basically got away from her.

'I wrote what I thought was half the book and suddenly realized that there was this huge, gaping hole in the middle of the plot,' she explained to *Entertainment Weekly*. 'The whole profile of the books got so much higher since the third book and there was an edge of external pressure.'

Joanne explained that the problem arose when she had to pull a girl character, a Weasley cousin, because she had discovered that this character was serving the same function as investigative journalist, Rita Skeeter.

Joanne was sorry if the delays or other editorial errors confused her readers and assured them that more care would be taken with future books.

Joanne arrived in Toronto on October 22, 2000. Her first order of business would be something personal. She had been in contact with Valerie McDonald and had arranged to spend some time with the McDonald family and Annie Kidder on that first day. After arriving in Toronto to no small amount of fanfare, and checking into her hotel, Joanne met with the McDonald family and Annie and spent what she would later state was a 'wonderful' afternoon of sightseeing at Niagara Falls. But while this time with friends put her in an upbeat mood, the fear of doing a reading in front of an estimated 20,000 adoring fans was once again on her mind.

'I'm so terrified,' she told the Knight Ridder News Service the day before the reading. 'I'm not The Rolling Stones. How is this going to work?'

The day before the Sky Dome reading was taken up with a number of interviews and meetings with representatives of her Canadian publisher. Joanne rather enjoyed meeting the press in Canada and patiently explained how her life had changed in the past few months since the publication of *Harry Potter and the Goblet of Fire*, retold some old stories about her early life that suddenly seemed fresh again, and dropped a few hints about the fifth Harry Potter book, already in progress.

During that busy day, Joanne also found the time to do some charitable work by appearing at a fund raising luncheon for the Toronto Public Library. And despite signs stating that no autographs would be given during the luncheon, Joanne once again missed a meal while she willingly greeted and signed books for a steady stream of children who approached her.

But the main point of interest continued to be the Sky Dome reading scheduled for October 24. Ticket sales had been reportedly brisk for the event and an estimated 20,000 fans would be in attendance. Joanne would acknowledge that she was delighted to be addressing so many of her fans at one time, but there was still a lot of nervousness at the notion of reading Harry in the middle of a huge baseball field.

'I'm kind of looking at it like, if I can get through this, I can get through anything.'

Joanne awoke the day of the reading with butterflies in her stomach. It was her big day.

The Sky Dome reading had been planned around a circus atmosphere. Children entering the stadium, many of whom were dressed as their favorite Harry Potter characters, were greeted by light shows and slide shows that projected elements of Harry Potter lore up on screens throughout the stadium as well as an indoor fireworks display. A group of outlandishly clothed wizards wandered through the stadium performing magic tricks.

Prior to Joanne's appearance, a pair of Canadian children's authors, Tim Wynne Jones and Kenneth Oppel, read selections from their most recent books. But it was obvious that the young fans in the stands were far more interested in hearing Joanne.

Finally the event announcer stepped to the podium. Before he could even get out her name, the crowd erupted in a wave of applause and cheers. The moment had arrived. The stadium lights dimmed and Joanne moved to the podium in the centre of the stadium and stood in the glare of a lone spotlight as the crowd went wild. The applause and cheers went on for some minutes as Joanne stood smiling and somewhat shocked at the response.

The thunderous applause continued as Joanne stepped up to the microphone. 'Thank you,' she said, her voice echoing through the stadium. 'I'm delighted and terrified to be here.'

The crowd went silent.

Joanne took out her copy of *Harry Potter and the Goblet of Fire*, laid it on the podium, opened it to chapter four, and began to read. Almost immediately, her young fans, many of whom had brought their own copy of the new book, did likewise and began to read silently along with her.

Her stage fright now magically gone. Joanne, reading clearly and occasionally adding dramatic voices and accents, brought life to passages in her book in which the Dursleys are visited by an assortment of wizards. The children sat wide-eyed and enraptured. Many had tears streaming down their faces. For them, this was truly a magic time.

Fourteen minutes after she began reading, Joanne was finished. She closed her book as the cheers once again cascaded down around her. For the next fifteen minutes, she offered up answers to the most frequently asked questions about Harry Potter and his world. She finished by thanking the audience for coming and stepped off the stage to thunderous applause and the voice of the announcer urging the children to 'read, read, read'.

Joanne was deliriously happy as she stepped from the stage, receiving congratulations from friends and associates for a job well done. She was literally on a cloud the next two days as she journeyed to Vancouver where she gave two more spirited readings before two sold out audiences at Vancouver's famed Pacific Coliseum and, whenever possible, reached out to the children who would shyly approach her.

Prior to those readings, Joanne once again sat down with a group of reporters, and she gave her reasons for agreeing to do a large reading like the one at the Sky Dome. She admitted that she would prefer the one-on-one contact that small readings and bookstore signings provided but that, sadly, those days appeared to be gone forever.

'If I did that now, I would never see my daughter,' she said in a story that is on the Harry Potter Fandom website. 'I would never write another book. I would never eat or sleep. So I have to cut my cloth. I could say, "Well, I won't read anymore," which I would really miss. Or I could do bigger readings where I reach more people at once and that's the way I've chosen to go.'

And while she told the assembled reporters that she considers books signings 'a bottomless pit' that often test her mental and emotional strength, she willingly does them and for one big reason.

'I've never had a rude child, which for me is incredible. Never had one throw a tantrum. I've never had a child ask for more than I can give. Never once had a child for which I didn't feel anything but affection.'

Joanne patiently answered the expected questions about dealing with success and what the future holds for Harry Potter. Although she would not like to have admitted it, Joanne was getting tired. And so she was grateful when the final round of applause greeted her last night in Vancouver.

Joanne knew it was time to go home.

She was missing her daughter terribly and, after six days of total adoration, was looking forward to returning to the simple life of writing at her favorite café, taking Jessica to and from school, and maybe doing a little shopping.

However, as her plane winged back across the Atlantic, she also knew there would be something else awaiting her. Something that both excited and scared her.

The movie version of *Harry Potter and the Philosopher's Stone* had begun filming two weeks earlier. And she could not begin to guess how a whole new world of Harry Potter would unfold.

11

IT'S ONLY A MOVIE

Joanne had flown to Los Angeles early in 2000 to finalise the contracts for the movie version of *Harry Potter and the Philosopher's Stone*. And for Joanne, seeing the place where movie magic was made was an eye opening experience. The negotiations were conducted in a cordial, straightforward manner in which Joanne's wishes were considered and honoured.

Joanne had been cautious in dealing with

the movie people. She had heard too many stories about books being totally distorted when adapted for the screen and was fearful of the same thing happening to Harry. But, in the end, Joanne came away from those meetings secure in the knowledge that the movie version of her book would be true to the world she created.

Joanne was given the title of executive producer when the deal was finalised with Warner Bros. to make the movie version of *Harry Potter and the Philosopher's Stone*. Knowing little about how the movie business worked, she did not think much of the title at first. But as the various elements of the movie began to fall into place, she was glad she had it.

Because, as often happens in Hollywood, suggestions were soon being made that would change *Harry Potter and the Philosopher's Stone* into something other than what the book had been. Early on, Steven Spielberg had been considered the front runner to direct the film. And Joanne had been thrilled with the idea of having the famed director of such films as *E.T.* and *Jurassic Park* create the Harry Potter world.

But during a series of meetings between Spielberg and Joanne, some very different opinions came to the surface. The director wanted to make a movie that would be more American, rather than English in tone. There was talk of making many of the students and teachers international. But Joanne strenuously objected on the grounds that doing that would mean inventing characters that were not in the book. Spielberg went so far as to suggest that child actor Hayley Joel Osment, an American, would be the perfect choice to play Harry.

In the end, Joanne and the director respectfully agreed to disagree, and Spielberg moved on to another project. There was immediate speculation that Joanne and the famous director did not get along personally. But Joanne, ever the diplomat, said that it ultimately boiled down to a question of whose vision would ultimately wind up on the screen.

'There were things he said that I didn't agree with,' she told the *Times*. 'There were things he said I did agree with.'

There were also questions raised early on about the kind of merchandising tie-ins that would accompany the release of the film. That there would be fast food restaurant toys, lunch boxes, dolls and fully licensed Harry Potter action figures associated with the movie was a sensitive issue with Joanne, who insisted that any merchandising connected with the film be tasteful and that a theme pushing literacy and reading be included.

Warner Bros. was agreeable to much of what Joanne said – typified by the fact that Coca Cola became an official sponsor of the film, but Harry would not be drinking a Coke in the film – and were in agreement that all associated items should be presented in a non-commercial manner.

Joanne insisted that, while she had basically sold the rights to let the studio do what they wanted, her opinion regarding the way Harry Potter was marketed had been taken into consideration by the studio. She had insisted, 'Please trust me. I am fighting in your corner,' when it came to how her creative 'baby' was being sold.

'If the action figures are horrible, tell the kids I said don't buy them,' she said in *Good Housekeeping*. The *New York Times* was also privy to the degree Joanne would defend her creation when she told them, 'I would do anything to prevent Harry from turning up in fast food boxes everywhere. I would do my utmost. That would be my worst nightmare.'

A number of other directors were offered up to Joanne until, early in 2000, Chris Columbus was finally named to direct the film. Columbus and Joanne were on the same page when it came to how *Harry Potter and the Philosopher's Stone* should be portrayed on the screen. They both agreed that, like the book, the film should be very British in tone and that it should be populated largely by British actors.

But when it was announced that American screenwriter Steve Kloves had been chosen to write the script for the movie, Joanne immediately had second thoughts.

'The person I was most nervous about meeting by far was Steve Kloves,' she related in an *Entertainment Weekly* interview. 'I was really ready to hate him. This was the man who was gonna butcher my baby. The first time I met him, he said, "You know who my favorite character is?" And I thought, You're gonna say Ron. But he said, "Hermione". I just kind of melted.'

Not too long after receiving the assignment to write the script, Kloves told *Reader's Digest* what he loved about Harry. 'From the first page of book one, she had me. There's a genuine edge and darkness to it, and one reason she's so popular with children is that there's no pandering whatsoever.'

He would recall in later months how the cordial relationship between Joanne and himself worked during the writing of the *Philosopher's Stone* script. He explained that much of the dialogue in the script was his variation on what Joanne had written in her book. In doing that, Kloves felt he was anticipating some elements of the ongoing Harry Potter story that would come into play in later books.

'She reacted strongly,' he reflected in an *Ain't It Cool* website interview. 'She was like, "Ah, you sensed something but you also missed something." In one instance, I put something in, a reference to something. She said, "That's great but you can't do that because something's going to happen in book five that makes that impossible ..."'

That Joanne would be such a stickler for

details does not come as a surprise, because Harry Potter, in the ensuing years, had become much more than a fictional character. 'I have known Harry and I have been writing about Harry for ten years,' she explained to the *Los Angeles Times*. 'He is very, very real to me.'

The year 2000 found Joanne burning the candle at both ends, putting the finishing touches to *Harry Potter and the Goblet of Fire*, while monitoring the progress of Kloves's first draft of the script and sitting in on meetings on other aspects of the film making process. With the director and writer in place, the next task was casting the film and, in particular, the all-important role of Harry Potter. The search for the perfect Harry was stretching worldwide with more than forty thousand child actors and just plain children auditioning for the role that would most certainly change their lives.

Joanne acknowledged that finding an

actor to play Harry was proving difficult and that finding an actor with the right look and acting ability was a challenge equivalent to the search that led to the choice of actress Vivian Leigh to play Scarlett O'Hara in *Gone With The Wind*.

'We'll know him when we find him,' she said to *Newsweek*. 'I am now walking around in London and Edinburgh and I'm looking at kids as I pass them, just thinking, Could be, you never know. I may just lunge at this kid and say, "Can you act? You're coming with me. Taxi."'

Initially the movie studio had hoped to get *Harry Potter and the Philosopher's Stone* into cinemas by summer 2001. But the combination of casting delays, lining up the incredible array of special effects and production design people necessary to bring the world of Harry Potter to the screen, and finding numerous London locations forced Warner Bros. to push back the release of the film to November 2001.

Casting the film was an ongoing challenge. Named actors as well as unknowns were being suggested for all roles. But midway through the year 2000, and a mere ten weeks before the start of filming, no actors had been cast.

Casting Harry continued to be the number one priority. More than 80,000 letters went out soliciting actors to audition and the casting directors visited more than 200 schools and numerous school drama departments. But the perfect Harry continued to be elusive.

Finally on August 21, 2000, it was announced that eleven-year-old Daniel Radcliffe had been selected to play the coveted role of Harry Potter. The young British actor, who had previously appeared in the film biography of *David Copperfield* and the drama *The Tailor of Panama*, was the spitting image of Harry Potter.

Joanne was ecstatic when she saw the youngster's screen test, feeling that after a long search, they had found their Harry. Director Chris Columbus was likewise thrilled.

'We saw so many enormously talented kids in the search for Harry,' he said in an announcement on the Harry Potter website. 'The process was intense, and there were times when we felt we would never find an individual who embodied the complex spirit and depth of Harry Potter. Then Dan walked into the room and we all knew we had found Harry.'

Radcliffe was officially presented as the film's Harry Potter in an August press conference. The youngster took easily to his new life in the spotlight as he patiently answered the media's questions.

'I cried and I was really excited,' he said in a *Hollywood Reporter* story. 'I think I'm a tiny bit like Harry because I'd like to have an owl. I am looking forward to filming.'

At the press conference, it was also announced that, since the movie would be titled *Harry Potter and the Sorcerer's Stone* in the United States and *Harry Potter and the Philosopher's Stone* in the rest of the world, a total of seven scenes would be shot two different ways to allow for the dialogue to include references to both titles.

Also, cast as Harry's closest friends were ten-year-old Emma Watson, as Hermione Granger, and eleven-year-old Rupert Grint as Ron Weasley. With the core trio of roles now cast, the remainder of the all-important supporting characters quickly fell into place.

They were: Sean Biggerstaff (Oliver Wood), David Bradley (Argus Filch), John Cleese (Nick The Nearly Headless Ghost), Robbie Coltrane (Hagrid), Alfie Enoch (Dean Thomas), Tom Felton (Draco Malfoy) and Richard Griffiths (Uncle Dursley). Also cast were Richard Harris (Professor Dumbledore), Ian Hart (Professor Quirrell), Joshua Herdman (Gregory Goyle), Matt Lewis (Neville Longbottom),

Rik Mayall (Peeves The Poltergeist), Devon Murray (Seamus), Katharine Nicholson (Pansy Parkinson) and Chris Rattling (Percy Weasley). Filling out the cast were Alan Rickman (Snape), Fiona Shaw (Aunt Petunia), Maggie Smith (Professor Minerva McGonagall), Verne Troyer (a ghoul), Zoe Wannamaker (Madame Hooch), Julie Walters (Mrs. Weasley) and Jamie Waylett (Vincent Crabbe).

Harry Potter and the Philosopher's Stone began filming in mid October 2000. It was cold in London as the cameras rolled for the first time. So cold that, when not shooting in the relative comfort of Leavesden Studios, heavy coats and hot water bottles was the order of the day.

As Joanne would find during her many visits to the set, her fears that Hollywood would do something bad to her story were unfounded. Under director Chris Columbus's direction, locations as diverse as Christ Church College, the reptile section of the London Zoo, Oxford University, the famed Australia House and Durham Cathedral had been magically transformed into delightful, larger-than-life landmarks of the Harry Potter world.

Throughout the production, Joanne would constantly, by telephone, email and fax, be kept abreast of any last minute script changes, casting additions and the film's progress in general. She happily reported to *Entertainment Weekly*, 'They [Warner Bros.] have been very gracious in allowing me input and I have been asked a lot of questions I never expected to be asked.'

Typical of the attention to detail involved in the filming process was the day at King's Cross Station, where Harry boards The Hogwarts Express for his fateful trip to The Hogwarts School. A steam engine made to look like Joanne's fantastic creation sat idling on the track, awaiting Harry's leap of faith through the platform barriers. On either side of The Hogwarts Express were platforms filled to overflowing with extras. Packed together on the platform were hundreds of child extras, many of them dressed in true-to-life Hogwarts uniforms, while others were wearing felt hats and cloaks. Scattered around the platform were luggage trolleys piled high with bags, trunks and broomsticks.

Amid the clutter of cameras, cables and crew people, director Columbus carried on an animated conversation with Daniel. There were smiles and laughs between them as Columbus instructed the actor on where to walk and how to look so he would be in the camera frame. Finally, the director called for action and the complex sequence of moving extras, trains and all manner of technical challenges unfolded in one continuous take as Harry approaches the train and makes the life changing decision to step aboard. The scene required a number of takes and the better part of a day to get right, but as the cast and crew wrapped up filming for the day, this important sequence was in the can.

Screenwriter Kloves, a frequent visitor to the *Philoshopher's Stone* set, came away with hints of other great moments. He claimed that sequences involving the flying broomsticks were 'amazing' and that scenes featuring Hagrid looked 'cool'.

Reports would continue to filter out of the top secret production that the actors were doing an excellent job of bringing Joanne's creations to life and that the production designers and special effects people were working their own magic to bring the Harry Potter universe to the screen. Joanne was heartened by the fact that her hopes for the film were finally being rewarded.

But the fantasy of filming *Harry Potter and the Philosopher's Stone* occasionally ran afoul of reality. Much of the movie was being shot in the middle of England's often wet winter and the movie makers would frequently have to shut down for the day because of rain. There were also some anxious moments when, because of his age and the laws regarding child actors, it was determined that, because of the delays, Daniel might not be able to finish the film. But after some careful negotiations, everybody had smiles on their faces and Daniel would be allowed to finish the movie.

The advance word on the film was so good that the movie studio announced that they had already approved the script for *Harry Potter and the Chamber of Secrets* and that filming of the second movie would begin before the end of 2001.

While *Harry Potter and the Philosopher's Stone* continued filming throughout the winter and into the summer months in London, Joanne was at home in Edinburgh and hard at work.

Joanne had never really had a timetable for completing any of her books in the early stages of her publishing career. Instead, with few distractions, she had been able to complete the first books in the Harry Potter series in just about a year per book. But, as the worldwide popularity of the books developed and the demand for her time increased, Joanne was admittedly having a hard time conforming to her normal writing schedule. Plus, in the back of her mind, she felt that taking the extra time might help avoid the delays and errors that plagued *Harry Potter and the Goblet of Fire*.

And so while she had hoped to have the fifth Harry Potter book out in time for the November 21, 2001 release of *Harry Potter and the Philosopher's Stone*, midway through the year Joanne would have to admit that she was not going to be able to complete the book. Her original goal had been to have Harry leaving Hogwarts as a fully-fledged seventeen-year-old wizard in 2003. But now that goal had been put in doubt.

Because there would not be a Harry Potter book in 2001.

12

INTO THE FUTURE

Word quickly spread around the world that *Harry Potter and the Order of the Phoenix* would not be published until sometime in 2002.

Fans were disappointed and more than a little bit frustrated at the prospect of having to wait more than a year for their next Harry Potter adventure. So were Joanne's publishers, who had been hoping to make a big splash with the new Harry Potter book coming out at the same time as the movie version of *Harry Potter and the Philosopher's Stone*. And her publishers did put some pressure on her to try and keep to the original timetable for the new book.

But Joanne stood her ground and refused to rush things.

'I really want to take my time and just make sure that it's as good as I can make it,' she told a Knight Ridder News Service reporter. 'I don't want to be running up against an artificial deadline. I'm working on it now and I have no intention of taking a break.'

To those familiar with Joanne's writing habits and attention to detail, it did not come as too much of a surprise that *Harry Potter and the Order of the Phoenix* was lagging behind schedule. Despite the fact that Joanne had long ago plotted out the seven books of Harry Potter, she had always prided herself on her ability to restructure the story and play either elements of her characters to the point where she was finally satisfied. Consequently, it took a year or more to complete each of the first four Harry Potter books.

But, according to close acquaintances, Joanne was suffering a bit of writer's fatigue based partly on the fact that she had, in hindsight, objected to the level of hysteria and secrecy surrounding the release of *Harry Potter and the Goblet of Fire*. In the aftermath of that experience, she was afraid that she would stop enjoying the writing process if she did not take a break and have a normal life.

So for a while, Joanne took things a little easier. She continued to write on a daily basis, but rather than pushing when she became tired or distracted as she had in the past, she would stop writing. Joanne would often take leisurely walks through the city, or make time to be with her daughter and with family and friends. This less hectic approach to writing agreed with her, and

Joanne would eagerly return to Harry each day with a new sense of excitement.

Now that it was common knowledge that Joanne was at work on the fifth Harry Potter adventure, the curiosity began to grow once again. Jessica would often return from school and tell her mother that the children were pestering her with questions about what *Harry Potter and the Order of the Phoenix* was all about. And it was a favorite topic of conversation in the handful of interviews Joanne did during this period.

Not surprisingly, Joanne had refused to give away too much information about the story line of book number five. But she had indicated that *Goblet of Fire* was the end of an era in Harry Potter's life and that *Harry Potter and the Order of the Phoenix* would point Harry's life in a totally different direction.

She hinted to the *New York Times* that Harry's 'innocence is gone,' that 'the mood may darken,' and that the death in book four is 'the beginning of the deaths' that may continue in the next book. She also hinted that, in book five, readers will discover why Harry returns to the Dursleys each summer and that Ginny Weasley, who had a crush on Harry in *Goblet of Fire*, will play a bigger role in the adventure. She also good-naturedly predicted that *Order of the Phoenix* will be scary, and that 'Harry finds out a lot of things he hasn't stumbled across so far.'

'Harry has already dealt with death,' she told a Canadian Broadcast Corporation interviewer. 'He lost his parents very young and in book four he witnessed a murder. So it is not news to anyone who has been following the series that death is a central theme of the books. It would be fair to say that in book five he has to examine exactly what death means in closer ways. But I don't think people who have been following the series will be that surprised by that.'

She also warned readers that book five

will see Harry's horizons broadening, and that he will be entering totally new areas of his magical world.

But while *Harry Potter and the Order of the Phoenix* would not come out for a while, there would be some new Harry Potter related books. Midway through 2000, Joanne came up with an idea to help fund one of her favourite charities, Comic Relief U.K. She agreed to write two 64 page books, both under a pseudonym, based on titles that appear in the Hogwarts library, with all proceeds from sales going to Comic Relief's Harry Potter Fund, which was formed with Joanne's cooperation to help fund children's causes.

The first book, *Quidditch Through the Ages*, is a fanciful, comprehensive guide to Quidditch and a resource guide to the magical world and its most popular sport. For this book, Joanne took the name Kennilworthy Whisp. The second book, *Fantastic Beasts and Where to Find Them*, is an

A to Z listing of all the fantastic creatures that populate the world of Harry Potter. Joanne wrote this book under the name Newt Scamander.

'I have always wanted to write these two books,' Joanne said in a press release announcing the books. 'I thought it was a wonderful opportunity to be involved in a charity I have always supported.'

Word quickly spread throughout Harry Potter fandom and the books were immediately snapped up upon their release in early 2001. Joanne would happily report that millions of dollars made from the sales of the two books had made their way into the Harry Potter Fund.

Joanne continued to use her writing for good works when she agreed to pen an original short story for a short story collection to be published in 2002 that would raise money for the National Council for Single Parent Families. Little was known about Joanne's contribution except that Harry Potter would not be in it and that its story, in keeping with the theme of the book, would be about some element of magic.

As 2001 came to an end, Joanne would plan to enjoy the holidays close to home and with family and friends. Christmas would see Joanne and Jessica enjoying a huge dinner with her sister and her family; a highlight would be watching her brother in law, a chef, cook up the holiday turkey. New Year would see Joanne and her daughter on holiday, taking in the sights and relaxing away from the constant demands on her time.

With her sister, Di, her family, and her close-knit circle of friends, Joanne could be assured of being treated as something other than a celebrity author. To these people, she was simply Jo and that was fine with her. Because, in her heart, Joanne was basically a shy personality who was still coming to terms with the celebrity status that Harry

Potter had brought her, to a large extent taking her away from the quiet life she had known. And while she now realized that she would forever be in the public eye, there was still a part of her that craved the privacy of a low profile life.

After the first of the year, Joanne would return to the reclusive life of a writer, insulating herself from outside distractions as she continued to work on *Harry Potter and the Order of the Phoenix*. She was once again excited as the adventure continued, first in her mind and then on the page, at a steady pace. For Joanne, writing *Order of the Phoenix* was a welcome return to the quiet times she had experienced before her simple tales of Harry Potter had catapulted her into the spotlight.

But she could not completely hide from the notoriety that went along with the fact that *Harry Potter and the Goblet of Fire* sold nearly 3 million copies in its first week and that there were nearly 50 million copies of her books in print in the United States alone. She had said that she had no idea if the worldwide mania for Harry Potter had reached its peak, and she is not sure if, even after four books, she has learned how to deal with the fame.

'I'm still learning,' she told a group of reporters while in Canada. 'I would definitely not say I'm on top of it. I would say that, for the first two years of it, I was in denial. I kept thinking it would go away. And about the time of the publishing of the third book, I had to accept the fact that it wasn't going away any time soon, which is probably a healthier place to be. It will go away. That's the nature of the game. And when it does I believe I will be happy. And I will have fond memories of the time I was famous.'

And the financial security that her fame had brought her. Joanne recently bought a second home in London, but anyone expecting her to spend her money frivolously on cars and helicopters, as was once speculated on in *Newsweek*, is sadly mistaken.

'Well, I can't drive so the five cars would be a problem,' she laughingly explained in response to *Newsweek*'s question. 'I don't want anyone thinking I'm a puritan. I enjoy spending money. But the main difference between where I was five years ago and where I am now is the absence of worry. I honestly believe that the only people who will really appreciate that are people who have been very, very broke. What I'm grateful for every day is that I'm not worried about the money.'

Money has always been a rather sticky subject with Joanne. It had been speculated often in newspapers and magazines about how much Joanne had made and how rich she was. Joanne had often refused to put an actual number to her riches. But she did recently state in a *Philadelphia Inquirer* interview that, 'I could not write anymore and never have to worry about not having money again.'

Joanne's notoriety and generous contributions to local charities had done much to make the author an unofficial ambassador for England and a favourite of the Royal Family. Early in the year 2001, Joanne was invited to their Gloucestershire country home for a meeting with Prince William, in which the heir to the throne complimented her on her books and her devotion to charity. On March 22, she was delighted and quite humbled when she had an audience with Queen Elizabeth on the occasion of a meeting between the Queen and members of the British publishing industry.

It was also during this time that Joanne fell in love with Dr. Neil Murray.

Not much was initially known about how the couple met or who the man was, but what was known was that whenever spotted walking hand in hand on the streets of Edinburgh, they seemed deliriously happy. Personally and professionally, Joanne appeared to be in a state of grace.

In terms of her chosen profession, she also considered herself very lucky.

'It (writing) has made me happier,' she said in a *Newsweek* interview. 'Finishing them (the books) has made me happier. It also makes me happy that the one thing I thought I could do, I wasn't deluded.'

And she was now looking to the future.

Uppermost in her mind was the future of the remaining books in the Harry Potter odyssey. Speculation was that book six would be titled *Harry Potter and the Green Flame Torch*, a rumour Joanne would deny. What she would speculate on was that she sees the remaining books as an exploration of the many personal and magical elements of Harry's character as he moves through his teen years. She saw the possibility of a romantic relationship for Harry and a more realistic interaction with the world around him. And while the final adventure of Harry Potter was still a few years off, Joanne was already looking forward to that finale.

'Book seven will be the biggest,' she predicted in a *Newsweek* interview. 'Seven is going to be like the *Encyclopedia Britannica* because I'm going to want to say goodbye.'

How she ultimately chooses to end the odyssey of Harry is still a mystery. Although she has acknowledged that she has already written the last chapter to the last book, doing so was mostly an act of faith to show that she really will get there in the end. Joanne is not quite sure what leads up to that moment. 'Besides I might just end up rewriting that chapter,' she joked during an online chat.

But, she offered the *Philadelphia Inquirer*, certain emotional elements of the final Harry Potter book were already in place. 'By the series end you feel a sense of resolution. You find out what happens to the survivors, to those characters who live through all seven books. I know that sounds very ominous.'

In the coming months, Joanne would remain the authority on her world as she oversaw the completion of the movie version of *Harry Potter and the Philosopher's Stone* and checked her email regularly for missives from screenwriter Steven Kloves, who was already hard at work on the script for *Harry Potter and the Chamber of Secrets*. In fact, Warner Bros. had recently finalised a deal for the film rights to all seven Harry Potter books, which meant that long after Joanne had written the literal last word on Harry, her legacy would be on the screen well into the next decade.

But with the self-imposed end of Harry Potter now in sight, Joanne looked at her creation with mixed emotions. 'I think when I've finished the seven Harry Potter books, I will be finished with the world,' she ventured in a Barnes and Noble online chat.

'It will make me very sad to say goodbye, but it must be done.'

Of course there were the rumours. The worldwide success of the Harry Potter books had been so massive that, reportedly, Joanne's publishers were hinting that it would be great if Joanne took Harry out of Hogwarts and into the world as a fully-fledged wizard. Although Joanne would publicly laugh off the notion of carrying Harry's adventures further than the projected seven books, she would occasionally tantilise a reporter with the notion that there were still stories that could be told.

'I always said that there would be seven,' she said in an *America Online* chat. 'If there's ever an eighth, it will be because, ten years down the line, I had a burning desire to do just one more. But I don't presently think that will happen. However, I think I might write a kind of 'Harry Potter Encyclopedia' and give the royalties to charity.'

And she indicated in the same chat that the notion of continuing to write children's books was also a possibility. 'I might write more children's books. I really don't know. I should say, however, that I do not feel I have to write my 'serious' adult book to be a 'proper' author. The idea comes first, not the target audience.'

Harry Potter and the Philosopher's Stone was scheduled to complete filming in the summer of 2001. Joanne, during her periodic visits to the filming, had been impressed and amazed at how her world was being translated from the page to the screen. The excitement continued into the fall as the publicity machine for the film switched into high gear. Everywhere she turned, she saw Harry or selected images from the film. The film studio was being cautious not to overpublicise the movie, but the early reaction to the bits and pieces of the film that were made available in cinemas and on television created an excitement around the coming movie that easily rivalled the arrival of each new Harry Potter book. As the days counted down to the November release of the film, Joanne could not help but find herself anticipating the movie, right along with her fans.

It was a good feeling.

'I'm going to be sitting there like everybody else, really wanting to watch Quidditch,' she told CNN interviewer Larry King. 'That's the thing I want to see most. I've been watching this thing inside my head for ten years so to be able to physically watch it on the screen will be wonderful. I feel like a kid when I think about it.'

13

REAL LIFE...FANTASY LIFE

*T*hat childlike feeling remained with Joanne through the days and weeks leading up to the November 2001 release of *Harry Potter and the Philosopher's Stone*. Finally, in October 2001, Joanne was told that the film was completed and a special screening of the film was scheduled for her. On the appointed day, she entered a screening room, settled into her seat and waited anxiously for the lights to go down.

Any concerns she had about how her literary child would be treated by Hollywood soon dissolved as she watched the images flicker across the screen. A smile appeared on her face that would not fade for days. Inside there was a sigh of relief.

Hollywood had got Harry Potter right.

'I'd say a week from seeing the film I was very excited,' she reported to a CBBC *Newsround* interviewer. 'And the closer the viewing came, the more frightened I became. When I actually sat down to see the film, I was terrified; because it was way too late if any of the bits were wrong. But at the end of the film I was happy. There's an awful lot of my book up there. All the important bits, I'd say.'

She would later state that she was particularly pleased with the way the actors had brought her characters to life and quite amazed at the way modern filmmaking and the wizardry of special effects had succeeded in making her most imaginative notions a big screen reality.

When *Harry Potter and the Philosopher's Stone* finally opened in November to rave reviews, Joanne was barely paying attention to the critical success the movie of her beloved book had become. The reason being that she was already hard at work on the latest installment of the Harry Potter series, *Harry Potter and the Order of the Phoenix*, and was already receiving anxious inquiries about when the next book would be completed.

Joanne was not a writer to be rushed, but she realized that with the first four Harry Potter books having been delivered on an almost yearly basis, her loyal fans had come to expect new Harry Potter adventures on a regular and timely basis and that she had, in a sense, spoiled them. But her feelings were that it would be giving less than her best effort to rush something out before she was satisfied that it was her best effort.

And besides, at the moment there was something that was equally, if not more, important to Joanne.

She was in love and she was preparing to be married.

For years Joanne felt that, with her struggles to make a life for herself and her daughter Jessica and her attempts to make a living as a writer, there was little time for love and romance in her life. And truth be known, while she had a beautiful daughter Jessica to show for her first marriage, the unhappy way it had ended was making her a bit shy about once again attempting a relationship and, possibly, falling in love. But, by 1998, with Harry Potter a worldwide success, Joanne told the *Sunday Telegraph*, 'I have what I always wanted. Now let's get Mr. Perfect in.'

Joanne was introduced to Dr. Neil Murray in the early part of 2001 at a party given by a mutual friend of both. She was immediately attracted to his boyish good looks, sly sense of humor and the fact that he was not awestruck by her notoriety. It also did not hurt that, with his slightly tousled dark hair, fully angular face and glasses, he bore a striking resemblance to her creation, Harry Potter, as a grownup. Was that part of the attraction? Only Joanne knows for sure. And she's not telling.

'The night we met, he told me he had read the first ten pages of *Philosopher's Stone* and he thought it was quite good,' Joanne recalled in a recent *Times* interview. 'And I thought that was fantastic. He hadn't read the books. He didn't really have a clear idea of who I was. It meant that we could get to know each other in a quite natural way.'

Joanne and Neil hit it off immediately and began dating right away. Getting to know Neil was easy. He was a good talker and a good listener. He had interests and a job that, like Joanne, he was passionate about. With Neil, Joanne could talk about anything or nothing and feel at ease. For Joanne, dating was an experience she had almost forgotten, but it returned in the ensuing months as their casual relationship, walking the streets of Edinburgh and dining at little out of the way bistros and pizzerias, turned quickly into love.

Neil and Jessica got along famously which, for Joanne, was the primary consideration in any personal relationship. And Neil's easy going nature was not threatened by the compromises that had to be made in their private time, when Joanne had to write or deal with other work connected to Harry Potter. It did not bother him when they were out and about and Joanne would be approached by people wanting her autograph or by children eager to talk to her about Harry. That lack of ego and security within himself made the young doctor even more attractive to Joanne.

Like everything else in her life, Joanne was adamant about keeping her relationship with Neil away from the public and the prying eyes of the press. But it was not long before the newspapers got wind of the man in Joanne's life and their relationship and their names became regularly linked in gossip columns around the world. Joanne was frustrated at the intrusion but knew it could not be helped and so she and Neil would adopt a humourous attitude toward their private life going public.

By July 2001, Joanne and Neil were head over heels in love and ready to be married. Knowing that any public ceremony would bring the press out by the hundreds and would destroy any sense of the quiet, private ceremony the couple wanted, Joanne and Neil decided that, during a secret, romantic cruise to the Galapagos Islands, they would sneak away and be married in secret. Plans were made and those few people who they wanted present at their wedding were notified.

Unfortunately the press found out about their plans and the normally sedate

Galapagos Islands were soon swarming with reporters and photographers. They placed inquiring calls to Neil's parents and to Joanne's publisher and agent. Joanne and Neil, feeling that their quiet wedding was about to turn into a media circus, called off the wedding plans.

For the moment.

But as the months played out Joanne and Neil fell deeper in love. She was on his arm at the premiere of *Harry Potter and the Philosopher's Stone* in November and it was at that time that the couple purchased the mansion in the town of Aberfeldy and made plans to make it their permanent residence once they were officially husband and wife. Their public appearances together and the growing knowledge by the world that Joanne and Neil were a couple meant their desire to be joined together in the eyes of God in marriage grew even stronger. Finally, as a Christmas present to themselves, Joanne and Neil decided to get married on December 26, 2001. And this time they were determined to avoid the prying eyes of the press.

To avoid any leaks, the couple asked a minister from outside the area they lived in to perform the ceremony. They went 50 miles outside of Edinburgh to hire the caterers for the reception that would follow the ceremony. A short list of 15 family, friends and relatives who would attend the ceremony were sworn to secrecy. And rather than a big church in the centre of Edinburgh for the ceremony, the happy couple chose to exchange vows in the hallowed halls of Killiechassie House, a mansion tucked away in the out of the way town of Aberfeldy.

On December 26, Joanne Kathleen Rowling and Neil Murray were united in marriage in a twenty-minute ceremony inside the cavernous halls of Kiliechassie House. Joanne's daughter Jessica served as one bridesmaid. Her sister Dianne and Neil's sister Lorna were also bridesmaids. Joanne, radiant in a cream colored wedding gown, had seen a big part of her fantasy life become a reality.

However the fantasy of that most perfect day would be short lived as reality once more entered their lives. Joanne was starting to feel the pressure to finish the latest Harry Potter adventure and conceded that she would not feel comfortable taking an extended honeymoon with that spectre hanging over them. And so the couple agreed that they would postpone their honeymoon until Joanne completed *Harry Potter and the Order of the Phoenix*.

Following the wedding, Neil returned to his practice while Joanne plunged eagerly into the task at hand, completing the book that the whole world was anxiously waiting for, *Harry Potter and the Order of the Phoenix*. There was a renewed sense of excitement and joy as the pages began to pile high. Joanne would occasionally drop little hints of what was to come in this latest installment of the Harry Potter odyssey. The fifth book would be approximately 800 pages long and would contain 38 chapters. There was the notion that, as characters grew into their teen years, the nature of their relationships would change and there was the persistent statement that at least one of the ongoing characters from the first four books would not survive to book six.

'It's dark,' Joanne hinted at during a 2002 BBC interview. 'There's a really bad death in it that I have not enjoyed writing.'

Joanne continued to tantalize readers when, during the odd press interview, she dropped further, often more detailed hints about what was to come in *Harry Potter and the Order of the Phoenix*.

In one interview she stated, 'The Dursleys are in the next book and there's stuff coming with them that people might not expect.' In another she reported, 'Harry will see the real Mad Eye Moody in book 5.' In yet another, she said, 'Why do some wizards become ghosts and the others don't? You will find out much more about that in book 5.'

Rowling seemed to enjoy dropping hints to her curious fans about what the future of Harry Potter would bring. In one interview, she hinted that the key to what would happen in the last three books could be found in *Harry Potter and the Goblet of Fire* when Dumbledore tells his students that they have to make a choice between what is right and what is easy. 'This is the set up for the next three books,' said Joanne. 'All of the characters are going to have to choose because what is easy is often not right.'

When a fan innocently asked the author what she would do if she was in Hogwarts for an hour, Joanne replied, 'I would go straight into a certain room mentioned in book four which has certain magical properties Harry hasn't discovered yet.'

Finally, as an aside to her characters now deep into their teen years, Joanne said

'They are 15 now and their hormones are working overtime. Something is going to go on between Ron and Hermione but Ron doesn't realize it yet. Typical boy.'

But the tidbits would only put fans off for so long and, as the weeks and months went by and the new book was nowhere near completion, the rumours began to circulate on a worldwide basis that Joanne had suddenly developed writer's block and was having trouble completing the book. Some had even suggested that married bliss with Neil was taking Joanne away from the task at hand. The book publisher, Bloomsbury and Warner Bros., the company producing the Harry Potter movies, had hoped for the perfect tie in, the movie version of *Harry Potter and the Chamber Of Secrets* and *Harry Potter and the Order of the Phoenix* coming out on the exact same day in November 2002.

However by May, with no manuscript completed, the rumours and fan patience turning to frustration, a public response was needed. Rebecca Salt, a spokesperson for Joanne, issued a short but concise statement that month that 'rejected any suggestion that Rowling was suffering from writer's block.'

But that did little to placate the fans who had by now calculated that it had been two and a half years since the last Harry Potter adventure. Joanne was giving few interviews at this point, preferring to concentrate on completing the new Harry Potter book. But, in a rare conversation with Newsround midway through 2002, she addressed the issue of the seemingly tardy book.

'There's a lot of the book done,' she said. 'That's all I want to say because if I give a date and then I pass it, everyone will be upset. I will say that I have a beginning, a middle and an end. You could read it all the way through and I know a lot of Harry Potter fans will say, "Just give it to us." But I'm a perfectionist and I want more time to tweak it. I have to laugh when I read bits about writer's block because I don't think I've ever been blocked in my life.'

Unfortunately such public statements did little to slow down the press. When there was no further news coming directly from Joanne, reporters began turning up in the town of Aberfeldy, asking people on the street, in cafes and other places of business if Joanne had been out and about and if they knew anything about her progress on the fifth book. The people were not talking. After the initial curiosity of having a world famous author living in their town, the townsfolk had warmed to Joanne and her family and their down-to-earth ways and became very protective of her privacy. So while the people of Aberfeldy knew nothing about Joanne and her writing life, even if they did they would not have said anything.

One secret that would be revealed in the following months was that, while reportedly writing *Harry Potter and the Order of the Phoenix*, Joanne was taking some time off to tackle another writing project, one she would later describe as 'a novel', possibly 'adult in nature' and something that, to this date, remains unfinished.

Joanne continued to use her popularity to do a number of personal and charitable good works. In April 2002, it was reported that Joanne had turned over the deeds to her old house in Edinburgh to a long time friend, Fiona Wilson. Wilson, also a single mother, had been a supporter and confidant of Joanne's during her struggling days.

A longtime supporter of single parent rights and funding, Joanne's voice was often raised in protest against the government's plans to cut funding for single parent services. She would make the point that trying to get by on government welfare is often a degrading situation for a single mother. Joanne pointed out that the depiction of her life as a single mother in her pre Harry Potter days was part and parcel of the problem of dealing with the needs of single mothers.

'Some articles written about me have come close to romanticising the time I spent on Income Support,' she told the *Daily Mirror*. 'The well-worn cliché of the writer starving in a garret is so much more picturesque than the bitter reality of living in poverty with a child. The reality was that I was humiliated by poverty.'

The writer also continued to be a strong and outspoken supporter of the plight of Multiple Sclerosis patients, the sad memories of her mother's slow and painful death from the disease still a harsh memory in her mind that would bring her sadness almost daily.

Joanne did more than talk about the problem of single parent families. With the cooperation of the British charitable organisation The National Council Of One Parent Families, Joanne was instrumental in putting together a fundraising short story collection, entitled *Magic*, to raise money for the organisation. The book features stories by such notable British authors as Sue Townsend, Fay Weldon, Jo Harris, Arabella Weir, Meera Syal, Ben Okri and Christopher Brookmyre. Originally Joanne had thought about writing an original short story for the collection. Eventually she changed her mind and, instead, decided to write a forward to the collection that would describe, in harsh detail, the often humiliating and degrading lifestyle she had led as a struggling single mother. *Magic* would ultimately earn more than £700,000 million for the charity.

While Joanne remained front and centre and very public in such causes, a sense of privacy would always enter into those small but no less noble causes that she involved herself with that would, inevitably, concern children who were sick or dying. And, because of her private nature, her good deeds would often not reveal themselves until weeks, months or years afterwards.

When a nine-year-old child named Abbey Cape had survived a near-death experience and a life saving heart transplant earlier in the year, Joanne, upon hearing of the young girl's plight, sent the young child a toy owl and a note of encouragement.

Easily the most heart wrenching encounter Joanne had ever had involved the plight of six year old New York native Catie Hoch. Catie, a loyal Harry Potter fan, had been diagnosed with a severe form of childhood cancer. Catie and her mother, Gina, were near the end of reading *Harry Potter and the Prisoner Of Azkaban* when the doctors revealed that the cancer was spreading and that young Catie only had weeks to live.

Catie, like all Harry Potter readers, was desperate to find out what happened next and her mother felt that any kind of contact with her favourite author would help ease her last days. A family friend sent an email to Joanne's publisher explaining Catie's story and asking if it would be possible for Joanne to get in touch with the dying child. Joanne was touched and deeply saddened and immediately sent off a personally written letter that she signed simply 'Jo'.

This began an email correspondence in which Joanne enthralled the sick child with bits and pieces of information on the latest book, *Harry Potter and the Goblet of Fire*, which she was working on at the time. Sadly, Catie's illness continued to progress and, at one point, it was determined that Catie only had days to live. Joanne made a fateful decision and arranged to call Catie personally and read whole segments of the yet to be published *Harry Potter and the Goblet of Fire* over the telephone.

Catie's mother Gina told the *Sunday Mirror*, 'We laid Catie down on the couch and Jo read to her over the phone. Catie's face lit up. I will be forever grateful for what Jo gave us. She gave us something priceless by having this relationship with Catie.'

Joanne called Catie and read to her on four separate occasions. Sadly the child's condition worsened and Catie died on May 18, 2000. Following her death, Joanne told Catie's parents that their little girl had left 'footprints on my heart.'

Throughout the months of 2002, Joanne, Neil and Jessica had settled into a rather quiet routine. Jessica, precocious but wise beyond her years, would be off to school. As she grew older, Jessica had learned to deal with having a celebrity mother and had turned out to be a level-headed, normal child. Neil was working steadily as an anesthesiologist at St. Johns Hospital in nearby Livingston. Joanne would occasionally do some window shopping in Aberfeldy and the family would take the odd couple of days for a holiday. But, for the most part, Joanne was hard at work on *Harry Potter and the Order of the Phoenix*.

Unfortunately the notoriety surrounding

her early writing habits made it impossible for her to go to a coffee shop, sit at a table, and write. But she had adjusted rather well to the well-ordered writing room in her new home. But she would admit in an interview with The Broughton High School magazine, *The High*, that she did indeed miss those quiet days of writing by hand at a table at The Nicholson Cafe with her then baby Jessica sleeping soundly at her feet.

'I still see a large cafe with a window seat as my ideal writing place,' she said. 'A large cafe with a small corner table overlooking an interesting street that would serve strong coffee and be non smoking.'

Work on the new book was proceeding at a steady pace. Joanne was encouraged by her progress; so much so that, during a mid-year interview with The *Times*, she answered, 'Probably' when asked about the possibility of the new book being out for Christmas. 'The manuscript is stacked nice, neat, pristine and big,' she added.

But the perfectionist in Joanne knew that the reality was that it would be a while longer until she had *Harry Potter and the Order of the Phoenix* where she felt she had done all the tweaking and fixing she could do.

During this time, Joanne was being kept abreast of the film of the second Harry Potter adventure, *Harry Potter and The Chamber Of Secrets*. Director Chris Columbus and screenwriter Steve Kloves were set to repeat their roles on *Chamber Of Secrets* and it gave Joanne much comfort that these experienced hands would once again be involved in interpreting her work. She felt the script for the second film was truly faithful to the book. She was also happy that, as in the first film, actors would come to her with any questions they had about how to play their characters. Joanne would receive progress reports from the set and was heartened by the continued use of traditional structures and locations in and around London and Scotland for the film.

Harry Potter and The Chamber Of Secrets had started filming three days after the first Harry Potter movie had opened in cinemas. Director Chris Columbus stated that he knew that *Chamber Of Secrets* would be a different kind of film.

'There are similar elements (to both films) but this one is a little darker, a little edgier and a lot more exciting,' Columbus told the BBC. 'One of the things we benefited from the second time around was that we'd set up the characters in the first film so we could immediately get into the story.'

The director also acknowledged that a big plus in the second film was that the main child actors were more confident and comfortable in their roles. 'They'd been doing it for 150 days on the first film and so they came to *Chamber Of Secrets* with a new found confidence and their performances were better.'

Like everyone else, there was a lot of curiosity on Joanne's part as she monitored the progress of the film.

The film's three child actors, Daniel Radcliffe, Emma Watson and Rupert Grint were now a year older. But so, she reasoned, were the characters in the book and therefore they would continue to be believable in the roles. The darker nature of *Chamber Of Secrets* was cause for momentary concern but Joanne quickly realized that the children who had read her books should have no problem accepting the fantastic and often nightmarish images on screen.

Joanne reflected on her lack of concern with how the movies would treat her books during an interview conducted with reporters from The Broughton High School magazine, called *The High*, shortly after the release of the movie version of *Harry Potter and The Chamber Of Secrets*.

'Originally, I was nervous about letting my books be made into films because I did not feel I was far enough into the series. I didn't want non-author written sequels where a film company could have taken my characters and sent them off to Las Vegas on holiday or something equally mad. I finally said yes when I knew I was far enough into the books to make it difficult for the filmmakers to take Harry and company in directions I didn't want them to go.'

It was at the point where the media attention for the movie was at its highest that the rumour surfaced that Joanne had secretly taken time off from writing and travelled to a well hidden movie location where she reportedly filmed a small cameo role for the movie. Joanne laughed when she heard it. It would be fun to do. But at that time she had neither the desire nor the time to play the actor.

Joanne continued to work on *Harry Potter and the Order of the Phoenix* throughout the winter and well into the summer months. The happiness of her married life was a constant boost to her spirits. Jessica had become the bright, intelligent young girl Joanne had hoped and prayed she would be. Neil, a hard working, dedicated and loving man, was always there for her in every way. But Joanne would have those days when even the warmth of family and home were not enough to put a smile on her face.

The pressure and expectation generated around the world for the coming Harry Potter book was hard to hide from. A pressure that became even more a part of her life when she realized that, despite her best efforts, she was not going to be able to finish the book for a hoped for December 2002 publication.

Adding to the stress was various new elements of the characters in the new book, especially Harry. Harry, Joanne would later report, was dealing with a lot of anger in this book and the first hints of teenage romance, which were challenging elements for Joanne. Also, Joanne had decided that she was going to kill off a recognisable character in *Order of the Phoenix*, a daring step in any case but one that is always a major risk in children's books. The stress of the death finally reached the breaking point one day when Neil found Joanne in the kitchen, sobbing uncontrollably.

'I had rewritten the death, rewritten it and that was it,' Joanne said in a story in The *Australian*. 'The person was definitely dead.'

Ever the supportive spouse, Neil suggested that if it was making her this upset, perhaps she should not kill the character. Joanne told him, 'Well, it just doesn't work like that. When you're writing a children's book, you need to be a ruthless killer.'

While writing Joanne was also reflective about the good and bad sides of fame that her creation had brought her. The good side was that she would never have a material need again, which meant lifelong security for her and her family. The downside was that her life as a successful author had put her permanently in the public eye and Joanne, who continued to be a shy and private person after years of obscurity, was not always happy with the idea of standing out from the crowd or the constant demands made on her free time. As always, Neil and Jessica were completely understanding of those demands and never complained.

Joanne continued to be frustrated at what she felt was an unnecessary intrusion on her family time and writing time and in 2002 she told a reporter for *Scotsman.com* about that frustration:

'There were times when I would gladly give back some of the money in exchange for the time and peace to write. That's been the biggest strain. I've become famous and I'm not very comfortable with that. Because of the fame, some really difficult things have happened and it's required a great effort of will to shut them out. There have been some black weeks when I've wondered whether it's worth it but I've ploughed on.'

Unfortunately, the task at hand seemed to become more difficult midway through the summer. Joanne was having a hard time focusing on the work and she was beginning to feel strangely out of sorts. A trip to the doctor confirmed what she already suspected.

Joanne was pregnant.

14

SECRETS REVEALED ...
LIFE GOES ON

Joanne was caught up in a swirl of emotions at the news. But one thing was certain ...

The tears that ran down her cheeks were tears of happiness.

Neil was thrilled at the news that he was going to become a father for the first time. Jessica was excited at the prospect of having either a younger brother or sister in the house. Once the initial rush of excitement died down, Joanne became once again practical in the face of this blessed event. She reasoned that announcing her pregnancy to the world this soon would only add to the pressure already on her because of the coming Harry Potter book, which by July 2002, was still not completed. Also there was the buzz surrounding the second Harry Potter movie, which was already being speculated on by the media as being so dark and scary that it might frighten much of the Harry Potter audience. And so she decided, quite logically, to hold off on an initial announcement of her pregnancy for a couple of months.

Joanne wrote at a consistent pace throughout the remainder of the summer as she fine tuned and added creative flourishes to a manuscript that would ultimately total more than 250,000 words. Joanne's thoughts, however, were never far from the baby slowly growing inside her stomach.

She daydreamed about the future and the joy and happiness that this new child would bring to their lives.

By September, rumours were already beginning to spread that the author of the Harry Potter books was pregnant and so she felt the time was right to make an official announcement. And so a spokesperson for Joanne, Nicky Stonehill, released a simple statement that said 'J.K. Rowling and Dr. Neil Murray are expecting a baby in the Spring'.

The response to the news was totally positive. The internet chat rooms were abuzz with questions of whether it would be a boy or a girl or what its name would be. It was around this time that one of the many rumours that always seemed to be circulating around Joanne and Harry Potter surfaced.

It was reported by a number of press sources that titles for the sixth, seventh and, yes, an eighth Harry Potter book had already been selected; the titles allegedly being *Harry Potter and the Pyramids Of Furmat*, *Harry Potter and the Chariots Of Light* and *Harry Potter and the Alchemist's Cell*. More amused than angry, Joanne told a BBC reporter 'No one, literally no one, not in my family or anybody else knows the titles to books six and seven and I'm going to keep it that way for now.'

Regarding a reported book eight, Joanne declared that she had no plans for Harry beyond book seven and, if she did do an additional Potter book, it would most likely be an encyclopedia of the Harry Potter world whose proceeds would go to charity.

Joanne had settled into a comfortable routine as she continued to polish *Harry Potter and the Order Of The Phoenix*. When not writing she would often find herself staring out the windows of her home into the quiet of the surrounding countryside and woods and reflect on the coming baby, her happy marriage to a wonderful man and the sheer wonderment that was watching

Jessica as she grew. She was a lucky woman. She was also a woman who continued to find ways of helping others.

As Halloween grew close, Joanne had braced herself for the endless parade of Harry Potter characters tramping through towns and cities all over the world in search of treats. She felt it a compliment but also thought that something should be done during this holiday season to help others.

Joanne had an idea ...To make Hogwarts a reality.

A series of telephone calls later and Joanne discovered that historic Stirling Castle in Scotland was available for functions. Under her expert guidance, Stirling Castle, with its deep hallowed halls and ancient pathways and ballrooms, was magically transformed into her fantasy institution, Hogwarts. Special invitations were sent out. For the sum of £250, one could spend a night in Hogwarts. The money was to be donated to a charity representing Multiple Sclerosis. And so on the night of November 1, 2002, invited guests were regaled by characters straight out of Harry Potter, wandering the castle. Assorted wizards and magicians plied their trade. A sumptuous dinner was held and an auction of Hogwarts-related items was held. All in all, a grand night for a good cause in which an estimated £275,000 was raised.

The next day was an important one for Joanne. She was excitedly primping and preparing herself for the London premiere of *Harry Potter and the Chamber Of Secrets*. Like the previous film, Joanne was again a flutter with a mixture of excitement, nervousness and curiosity. For her, the same questions needed to be answered all over again.

Needless to say, that night Joanne, on the arm of Neil and five months pregnant, was radiant as she walked down the red carpet at the Odeon Leicester Square in London, through an unexpected rainstorm, smiling nervously as the expected press photographers cameras clicked away in a constant explosion of flash bulbs. But as she bravely stood, allowing the press their photos, a smiling and supportive Neil at her side, she looked past the photographers and was amazed …

Lines of fans had shown up at the premiére, with no hope of getting in the theater, wearing outrageous costumes and all done up in Hogwarts colors. She waved enthusiastically to them before entering the cinema.

People magazine reported that Joanne, that night, was heard to remark, 'I didn't think it would ever be this mad. When I wrote the book it would have been insane for me to imagine all this.'

Once again she was hopeful as the lights dimmed. Once again she was rewarded. Chris Columbus and Steven Kloves had once more worked their magic as Harry and his world came alive on the screen. The characters had continued to grow and mature. The scary bits were scary enough, but not too scary. Hollywood had once again captured the magic of her books and her fertile imagination.

In fact, Joanne was so happy with the film that she overcame her shyness and willingly stopped to talk with the media after the screening. And it was at that point that a BBC reporter managed to get the information that the entire world had been waiting so long to hear.

'I'm putting the finishing touches on the manuscript,' she said. 'I'm weeks away from delivering it to the publisher. I'm really pleased with it. I'm just going to tweak it a tiny bit more and then the publishers will have it.'

True to her word, the completed manuscript for *Harry Potter and the Order Of The Phoenix* was turned over to Bloomsbury during the first days of December 2002.

Encouraging children to read continued

to be one of Joanne's main cultural crusades and she used that cause as an excuse to tantalise her fans with snippets of what was to come with her latest book. Joanne penned a 93-word document in which she revealed some of the plot of *Harry Potter and the Order Of The Phoenix*. She turned the document over to the famed London auction house Sotheby's to be auctioned off on December 12, with all proceeds going to Book Aid International. Word quickly spread about this highly collectable item and the bidding was spirited on the day of the auction. When the gavel finally came down, the document had been sold for $45,300 to an American collector whose identity was kept secret.

With *The Order Of The Phoenix* behind her, Joanne suddenly had quite a bit of free time. Much of it was devoted to Jessica and preparing for the arrival of her second child. Joanne could also often be found in the Harry Potter Internet chatrooms, sending and receiving thoughts and impressions of the Harry Potter universe, under a false name, with children. Joanne had become familiar with the Internet while writing her second book, *Harry Potter and the Chamber Of Secrets*, and became fascinated with the notion of communicating through cyberspace.

'Typing your thoughts into the ether and getting answers back, you don't know who is answering you.'

Joanne was also using this time to get off by herself for a few hours, usually to go into Edinburgh for a bit of shopping or to do some errands. It was during these moments that she would often dress rather informally and very unlike the image that had grown up around her as a prim and proper writer. Joanne would usually go unnoticed during these trips but, according to a *People* magazine article, she was spotted one day by a local journalist wearing rather outrageous attire.

'She was dressed in high heels, black pants, an animal print jacket and puffed up hair,' reported Scott Doughlas. 'I thought to myself, that's J.K. Rowling. She's obviously got a vampish side.'

Unfortunately the price of fame would soon cause Joanne some discomfort. With her worldwide popularity, she soon found herself the target of overzealous and obsessed fans whose attention and correspondence regarding her every waking moment soon became unsettling. Sadly, with the protection of her family and herself uppermost in her thoughts, Joanne, in 2002, had eight-foot high walls, topped with electrical wiring, built around her home.

But things were not all strident and serious in those months. Long a fan of *The Simpsons* television series, Joanne was approached by the show's creator Matt Groening to appear in an episode of *The Simpsons* that had the cartoon family travelling to England and running into J.K.

Rowling at a bookstore where they exchange comic pleasantries with the author. Joanne readily agreed and had quite a bit of fun recording her dialogue for the episode entitled *The Regina Monologues* that aired late in 2003 to rave reviews.

In her final month of pregnancy, Joanne continued to be encouraged by the reports she was receiving about the earliest days of filming of *Harry Potter and The Prisoner Of Azkaban*. Filming had officially begun on February 24 at Leavesden Studio in London and would continue in lavish outdoor locations in London and Scotland. Joining the returning cast from the previous films were newcomers Gary Oldman, who plays Sirius Black, Michael Gambon as Professor Dumbledore, Timothy Spall as Peter Pettigrew, David Thewlis as Professor Lupin, Pam Ferris as Aunt Marge and Paul Whitehouse as Sir Caddogan.

As production began, director Alfonso Cuaron beamed with pride as he told the press, 'To be entrusted with such rich and beloved material, and to be given the opportunity to collaborate with this extraordinary cast and crew on the next Harry Potter adventure, is an honour. I look forward to bringing this intricate story to the screen and sharing it with film audiences around the world.'

The enormity of the production, with its trademark special effects and scenes with literally hundreds of extras in them, was going to be a long, complex production. And so while the first two films had been right on time for a Christmas release, the studio knew better than to rush the film out and so announced early in the production that *Harry Potter and the Prisoner Of Azkaban* would not be released until early 2004 (perhaps February or March) but most likely not until May or June 2004.

The past year, which Joanne would describe in a *Sunday Herald* interview as 'hellish and massively stressful', had given way to a period of quiet reflection and solitude as Joanne waited for the blessed event. She was already working on early elements of the sixth Harry Potter book but was finding it difficult to focus on the task at hand. In a rare correspondence with a fan, *Wizard News.com* reported that Joanne told the young child, 'It's really strange writing the book now that I'm pregnant.'

But while her obligations to Harry continued to demand her attention, Joanne was, overall, in a comfortable state during her last months of pregnancy. According to an interview with Barbara Murray, Neil's mother, in *People*, 'She is relaxed and glowing. She's looking so very happy with the new baby coming and the marriage going so well.'

Those in her immediate circle knew that, despite the marriage, the coming baby and the worldwide notoriety that continued to grow because of the success of her books, very little had changed in Joanne's attitude to life.

'Rowling still has her feet on the ground,' reflected her publicist Rosamund de la Hey in a *People* article. 'Her life has changed very little in day to day ways, apart from the obvious financial security she now has.'

Shortly after the first of the year, Joanne's publisher announced that *Harry Potter and the Order Of The Phoenix* would be in stores on June, 21, 2003. Not long after that announcement was made, Joanne went into labour.

Joanne was driven by Neil to the New Royal Infirmary's Simpson Centre For Reproductive Health on Sunday March 24. Not long after entering the hospital, David Gordon Rowling Murray, weighing in at a little more than eight pounds, was born. The birth of Joanne's second child was of worldwide interest but it was the local Scotland papers, such as the *Edinburgh Evening News*, who were there first with all the facts.

Shortly after the birth, Nicky Stonehill, speaking for Rowling, announced the birth and added, 'Both mother and baby were doing well.'

Neil's mother, Barbara Murray, was one of the first to talk publicly about the birth of her grandchild when she was quoted in the *Edinburgh Evening News* as saying, 'I've seen David and he is gaining weight, more than eight pounds at the moment. Both Joanne and the baby are doing well. We're all just highly delighted.'

After a short recuperation period, Joanne and the baby were brought home by proud father Neil amid tight security around the home. The few friends and family members who were allowed into the home to see the newborn had to pass through a checkpoint in which names were matched with a very short list of who would be allowed inside.

Joanne had already stated that, with *Order Of The Phoenix*, she would not go through the kind of publicity tour that accompanied her last book and so, with the birth of David, her publisher announced that she was planning on making fewer press appearances and that there would be no long book tours. An official statement from her publisher further stated that the baby would only be three months old when the book is published and, like any new mother, she wants to enjoy the time. In a related press statement, Joanne said, 'It's a very important time for me and my husband and we want to spend as much of it as we can with the baby and Jessica.'

Joanne spent the next few weeks largely in seclusion, spending almost all her waking hours with the baby. Her natural loving, maternal instincts were very much in evidence as she soothingly cooed to the baby and comforted her bundle of joy. Their quiet moments together were often taken up with long walks through the mansion. Joanne would stop, look out a window and introduce her young son to the world around her. At that moment, work was the farthest thing from her mind.

But her absence from the public eye did not prevent the world of Harry Potter from continuing to turn.

Joanne's US publisher, Scholastic, in their summer preview catalogue, unveiled the plot synopsis of *Harry Potter and the Order Of The Phoenix*. It read: Lord Valdemort's rise has opened a rift in the wizarding world between those who believe the truth about his return and those who prefer to believe that it is all just madness and lies. Harry confronts the unreliability of the government of the magical world and the impotence of the authorities of Hogwarts.

In April, a press conference, covered by BBC and other media outlets, was assembled to announce the release of the *Harry Potter and the Chamber Of Secrets* on DVD. But as these kinds of events often happen, the real news was the tidbits of information that were revealed about the Harry Potter movies to come.

Film producer David Heyman announced that *Harry Potter and The Prisoner Of Azkaban* had been in production in and around London and the British countryside since February and that the production was right on schedule. As an example of what Harry Potter fans could look forward to on the big screen, Heyman explained how the film company had recently completed a scene in the Gryffindor Common Room where Professor McGonagall is angry at Neville after finding out that he had left the password list lying around.

Robbie Coltrane, who has played Hagrid in the previous two Harry Potter movies, said that there was something new on the horizon for his character in the new film. 'Hagrid has a new look,' he said at the press conference. 'He's got a waistcoat. His clothes are looking more like he made them himself, which, indeed, I'm sure he did.'

Producer Heyman also revealed that writer Steve Kloves was already hard at work on the script for *Harry Potter and The Goblet of Fire*. He indicated that while that script was being written with the idea of it being one movie, there was the possibility that, because of the length and complex nature of the story, *Goblet of Fire* might end up being made into two movies. Heyman reported that *Goblet of Fire* would most likely go before the cameras sometime in 2004 and that the movie would be released a year to a year-and-a-half after the release of the third film.

Uppermost in the minds of many has been the fact that the child stars of the Harry Potter films were getting older and that there might be a point when the actors will have outgrown the part. Heyman addressed the question of whether *Prisoner Of Azkaban* might be the last time in Harry Potter's world for Daniel Radcliffe, Emma Watson and Rupert Grint.

'My hope is that it would be the same cast. But it's too early to tell, though.'

Another rumour, addressed by Chris Columbus at the press conference, was whether the director of the first two Harry Potter movies would be back to direct the fourth. Columbus, who bowed out of directing *Prisoner Of Azkaban* to spend more time with his family, indicated that while 'Four was starting a little too soon, five is a possibility.'

By early May, the completed manuscript for *Harry Potter and the Order Of The Phoenix* had been edited and, amid tight security measures that one usually associates with a visit from royalty, the manuscript was driven to the printing plant, Clays Ltd. in the nearby town of Suffolk where the first issues of Joanne's new book would be printed. Rumours, almost as fantastic as Joanne's books, began to circulate.

One widely reported rumour had it that crates containing the new books would not be delivered until the day before the publication date and that the books would be brought in by armed guards. One story that turned out to be true was that, after the book was edited, Joanne and her publisher reportedly sent sketches of what they wanted the book cover to look like to the cover artist, Jason Cockscroft, rather than letting him see the book and generate his own ideas. One person who did get an advance look at the book was Mary Grand Pre who created the illustrations for inside the book and had to read the entire story before she did her work.

Around this time there was rabid speculation about whether Joanne had let Neil or her daughter Jessica get a sneak peak at the book. Many assumed that both her husband and her daughter had been monitoring the work in progress and may well have read some, if not all of the book already. But nobody could be sure.

Review copies to influential authors were also being handed out with extreme care and with the warning that their might be dire consequences if reviews ran too soon or if too much of the story was given away too far in advance of the publication date.

For many, these precautions might appear to be a bit much. However, with the worldwide popularity of Harry Potter, with recent books stories had emerged of people attempting to steal copies of the manuscripts and sell them to certain media outlets and thus destroying the surprise for devoted readers. Joanne had no problem with these precautions.

But despite the security, Joanne's worst fear would come true during the second week of May 2003.

Keith Webb, an unemployed truck driver, was walking through a field in Suffolk when he happened to look down and spotted what appeared to be a couple of old, coverless discarded books. In an interview with the *Sun* newspaper, Webb would relate what happened next.

'I wondered what it was and bent down to pick them up. I was astonished when I read the front page and saw that it was copies of the latest Harry Potter book.'

What had tipped Webb off was that the first page contained the title *Harry Potter and the Order Of The Phoenix* and Joanne's name. Webb also saw that the dedication page read 'To Neil, David and Jessica who make my world magical.'

Surprisingly, Webb's first thought was to call the *Sun* and report his finding. Webb eventually turned the copies of the book over to the newspaper. Even more surprising was the action of the *Sun*, a paper often known for dabbling in gossip and sensationalism. The newspaper editors locked the books up for safe keeping, would not let anybody read them and called Joanne's publisher to come and get them.

When Joanne heard the news she was extremely upset and then relieved when she found that the books had been returned, apparently unread. However her concerns resurfaced when it was reported that the *Sun* and several other publications had received mysterious telephone calls from someone offering to sell them the first three chapters of the new book for a large amount of money. The publications all refused the offer but there remained the fear that at least one other copy of *Order Of The Phoenix* was in the hands of somebody who was trying to ruin the surprises the new book had to offer.

The Suffolk police stepped in and began investigating the apparent theft of the copies of the book from the printer. There was a collective sigh of relief a few days later when a 44-year-old man was arrested and charged with stealing copies of chapters of the novel and a pair of teenage boys were arrested and charged with handling stolen goods.

Joanne was sorry that these people had used the idea of making money from her manuscript to enter into a life of crime. But she was relieved to discover that millions of children would still have the surprise of opening *Harry Potter And The Order Of The Phoenix* and reading those opening pages. Once more she reflected on the price of fame and that bad things sometimes happened in connection with her work. Unfortunately, there was little she could do to prevent these things from happening and so she chose to put the negative aspects out of her mind and concentrate on all the good things.

As the days counted down to the June 21 release date of *Harry Potter and the Order Of The Phoenix*, bookshops around the world prepared for the new book with a variety of parties and readings centred around the world of Harry Potter. Many shops had arranged to begin selling copies of the new book at the stroke of midnight. But Joanne continued to state that she would make very few press appearances. And what she would do, while not on the massive scale of her previous reading tour in Canada years earlier, would be for the benefit of children.

Joanne agreed that on June 26 2003, five days after the publication of *Harry Potter and the Order Of The Phoenix*, she would appear at the famous Royal Albert Hall in London to read from and answer questions regarding her latest book. The audience would be made up of 4000 children who would be selected through a contest run by both her British and US publishers.

But beyond that appearance, Joanne was insistent that they would see little of her or her new baby which, nearing two months old, was nowhere near ready to be out in public.

The weather in Scotland in May can go from sunny and warm to rainy and cold in the blink of an eye. Nowhere was this more apparent than in the rolling hills and deep forests of Glencoe in Northern Scotland where much of *Harry Potter and the Prisoner Of Azkaban* was being filmed.

Outdoor   scenes   in   which   The

Executioner pays a visit to Hagrid's Hut had to be postponed for three days because of rain. The resourceful filmmakers got around this act of God by filming the interior elements of these sequences at nearby Fort William. When the rain finally gave way to sunshine, director Cuaron moved the production back outside where, over the course of a number of days, they filmed the aforementioned scenes around Hagrid's Hut and, with the film's three stars leading well over a hundred child extras, a number of scenes involving Hogwarts Castle were also completed.

David turned two months old at the end of May. It was a time of happiness and quiet expectation. In a relatively short time, Neil had grown to be the ideal father, attentive to the needs of his son and eager to spend time alone with him when Joanne needed to rest or some time to write. Jessica adored her younger brother and would spend every free hour playing childlike make-believe games.

Joanne was continuing to work on the sixth Harry Potter book but was doing so at a more leisurely pace. No longer willing to race through the ever more complex storylines in an attempt to satisfy her publisher's need for a new book every year, Joanne had publicly announced that she would be taking more time with the next book and that readers will most likely have to wait until sometime in the year 2005 for the next Harry Potter adventure. There was some disappointment when Joanne made that announcement but most of her fans eventually came to realize that they had to be patient in order to get the best Harry story that Joanne could possibly write.

Joanne was feeling a wide variety of emotions as she realized that, in writing the sixth Harry Potter adventure, she was nearly finished with the promised seven book odyssey. By the time that last book was completed, Harry would be 18 years old and ready to go out into the world. And what of

Joanne at that point? Materially she would never want for anything and could, if she desired, stop writing and never have to work again. But Joanne often rationalised that writers live to write and, while she did not know for sure what she would do after Harry, she was sure that she would be writing something.

Harry Potter mania began to shift into high gear during the early days of June. Bookstores and websites were counting down the days, the hours and, yes, even the seconds. Newspapers and magazines were filled with stories covering every aspect of Joanne and the arrival of her latest work. One story proclaimed that at the stroke of midnight on June 21, nearly 9 million copies of *Harry Potter And The Order Of The Phoenix* would be released in the United States alone. A report from Ireland indicated that sales of the coming new book would easily outdistance sales of the *King James Bible*. A library in Oregon made worldwide news when they reported ordering 700 copies of *Harry Potter And The Order Of The Phoenix* in order to accommodate more than 1000 requests that had already come in.

Joanne continued to be amazed at the amount of attention being given to her creation. But then she would hear the cries of her child who craved attention on a level that only a mother could understand. And moments like that reminded Joanne what was really important.

One of the things that amazed Joanne most were the recent polls conducted in England and Scotland which focused on the most rich and powerful people in the country. In a poll conducted by the *Sunday Times*, Joanne found herself near the top of the list of the wealthiest people in England, an astounding eleven places higher than Queen Elizabeth. And, in a list of Scotland's 100 most powerful people, Joanne came in at number four.

Joanne looked at these lists and found it

hard to believe that she was on them. In many ways that person was not real to her. After all, just a few short years ago, she was a single mother living on welfare in a drafty flat. Now she had mansions and a loving family around her. It was a fantasy come true. But she was proud that, with all the accolades that had come her way because of Harry, she had kept to her values. She knew how money and power causes many people to change for the worse once they come into the public spotlight. And she knew that she was not one of those people.

Joanne agreed to do a few interviews in the weeks and days leading up to the publication of *Harry Potter And The Order Of The Phoenix*. Because of the nature of the interviews she had done with the release of her previous four books, Joanne had come to expect a certain line of questioning that she felt more than capable of answering. But she soon realized that a lot had happened in the previous two years. So while a good part of the interviews centred on the new book, a lot was asked about her new baby, her husband and a lot of things she considered highly personal. True to her private nature, Joanne would respond to those questions with vague or simplistic answers, refusing to go into any grand detail. She was grateful that even the more gossip oriented reporters did not push her really hard for personal information and even happier to find that the often jaded reporters maintained a high degree of enthusiasm for the coming of *Harry Potter And The Order Of The Phoenix*.

With all the incredible excitement surrounding the coming release of *Order Of The Phoenix* that often, reasoned Joanne, seemed to focus more on the material aspects of the books than the joys inherent in the stories themselves, she was quite heartened to discover that one of her many fans was turning his interest in Harry Potter to charitable use. Adam Orton, a 15-year-old English lad, had raised more than one thousand pounds for the Children's Liver Disease Foundation by auctioning off several signed Harry Potter books.

During this period, Joanne continued to get progress reports on the filming of *Harry Potter And The Prisoner Of Azkaban* in nearby Glencoe. And the reports were not always good. An unexpected fire had halted the proceedings for several days and the continuing rain, mud and the constant presence of flies had resulted in the production being two weeks behind schedule. At one point, things got so bad that the actors had to be transported to a hill top location in a snow mobile. To make matters worse, filming in and around the outdoor location of Hogwarts bridge had become so bad that the entire prop bridge had to be taken down and rebuilt inside a London soundstage.

Still, she was heartened to learn that, despite these setbacks, a firm release date for the film of June 4, 2004 had been announced. On the other hand, she was quite surprised that it was already being stated in many press outlets that Warner Bros. was planning on making two movies out of the sixth Harry Potter book. The sixth book was nowhere near completion so Joanne was curious as to how such a statement could be made. But she decided to not let these stories get in the way of her life and her work.

Joanne continued to be consumed with David. It had been a number of years since she had dealt with the everyday requirements of a newborn and was finding unbelievable joy in the most mundane of moments. The chores of feeding, cuddling and changing helped fill her days and helped settle her nerves as she anticipated the arrival of her next blessed event. By this time, Joanne had become accustomed to all the attention that came along with the publication of each new Harry Potter book and, she reflected, nothing could ever erase the memory of the publicity tour that accompanied the release of *Harry Potter And The Goblet of Fire*.

But a lot of questions had been asked this time around of her, and her creation, and Joanne admitted to herself that *Harry Potter And The Order Of The Phoenix* was a turning point for her characters and her career. The adventures of Harry would end in a relatively short time and then she would be faced with the question of what she would do with the rest of her life. And while she felt confident that the new book would be a smashing success, she was already looking to the future...

And it was a future in which she did not have all the answers.

Finally the day arrived. The world had been counting down for months, then weeks, then days, then hours. Around the world lines were beginning to form outside bookstores; anxious children and just as anxious parents. Inside the books were being piled high, their fantasy covers aligned to welcome fans to Joanne's continuing fantasy.

At the stroke of midnight on June 20, 2003, the doors opened. Minutes into the new day, millions of readers were already opening the book and the adventure was once again beginning to unfold.

Despite her insistence that she would not do any appearances other than the Royal Albert Hall reading, Joanne, on the day *Order Of The Phoenix* was published, had an unexpected change of heart and, shortly after the books went on sale, appeared unannounced at a local Edinburgh bookstore where she happily signed copies of her new book and talked to the surprised and delighted children.

Harry fans were so excited that they could not wait to get the book home and were sitting, alone or in clusters, reading silently or in excited twos and threes around the bookstore. It soon became an informal contest to see who could read the book the fastest with a young college student reportedly finishing the book in 104 minutes. Over the next days, there would be endless stories surrounding the publication of the book. The first reviews were not long in coming and were all fairly unanimous in their praise of the book; making particular notation of the complexity and depth of the story and the believable way in which Harry and his companions had grown up. It was also touched on, in a positive sense, that *Order Of The Phoenix* was the darkest book yet.

All available copies of *Harry Potter And The Order Of The Phoenix* were quickly snapped up and, despite the thousands of copies ordered by many stores in preparation, many soon found themselves running low or completely out of copies of the book in a matter of days and were placing frantic orders for more books to keep up with the demand. Likewise the printers were working around the clock, printing up more and more copies in an attempt to keep up with the worldwide outcry for more books.

Much controversey and debate surfaced when it was discovered that it was Sirius Black, a close friend of Harry's, who was killed. But finally the long anticipated death was felt to be a satisfactory, albeit unpleasant decision.

Joanne was thrilled with the response and not just the slightest bit relieved as she received the good news that her book had immediately jumped to number one on a number of the most prestigious best seller lists. But it did not take long for the nerves to return when she realized that her reading at the Royal Albert Hall was only a few days away.

Joanne had been forced to overcome her shyness in promoting the previous books and looked back in pride on her ability to command an audience of thousands in the

Canadian sports stadium and in smaller but equally crowded rooms during the promotion of the last book. But now, some of the old fears and discomfort of speaking in public had returned. There were a million other things she would rather be doing but, once she reminded herself that she would be speaking in front of children who were her biggest supporters, the nerves began to disappear.

But she remained in an excited state on the day she travelled to London for the Royal Albert Hall appearance. She rarely went into London now except for business reasons and so she was once again enchanted by the sights and sounds that greeted her.

She was not surprised to find that the scene outside the hall was similar to those that had followed her every public appearance since Harry Potter had put her in the public eye. Thousands of children and, yes, adults, were being politely but firmly held back behind barricades by the local police. Many in attendance were dressed as their favourite Harry Potter character and many held copies of the new book. Through an elaborate security set up, those lucky children who had won the coveted tickets to the event were being allowed in.

Joanne entered the Royal Albert Hall through a backstage entrance where she waited in the wings for a formal introduction. As she looked out into the packed hall, memories of her last big appearance in Canada came rushing back to her. While on a much smaller scale, the Royal Albert Hall was electric with excitement as children from places all over the map chattered excitedly as they embraced this special moment and awaited Joanne's appearance.

Just when it seemed that the noise level could not get any higher, Joanne was introduced. Screams and cheers of joy greeted Joanne as she walked to centre stage. She smiled, a deep satisfied smile. Any sense of nervousness melted away as 4000 children expressed their love for her and what she had brought to their lives.

Joanne thanked them for coming and, after a few introductory comments, commenced to read a passage from *Harry Potter And The Order Of The Phoenix*. Many in the audience had their own copies of the book open to the appropriate page and were reading along, silently and, in some cases, aloud, with her. Another round of applause and cheers roared up as Joanne looked up from her book, finishing her reading.

Joanne followed up the reading by answering questions from the moderator and from the audience. She would later acknowledge that she was amazed at the earnestness of the questions. The children wanted to know why this book had taken so long to write, why she had decided to take characters in the directions she did, what the future books would be like and what she thought of the movies. There was also the occasional question about the new baby and her family which, as they were coming from children rather than the press, she answered.

Joanne left the stage to thunderous applause. Her heart was beating a mile a minute. The children were the people she wrote the Harry Potter books for. This demonstration of their approval of what she had done was all the praise that she needed.

Now it was back to the warmth and comfort of her family.

With the uproar over her latest book continuing, Joanne retreated to a simple home life, taking care of baby David, looking after the needs of Neil and Jessica and, for the first time in a long time, writing without the pressure of deadlines. After the stress she suffered writing *Goblet of Fire* and *Order of the Phoenix* literally back to back,

Joanne came to an agreement with her publishers that the last two books would be delivered in their own time and they agreed.

Although mum on the particulars of her current progress, Joanne did tell *The Times* that 'book six will be shorter than *Order of the Phoenix,*' but that, 'the final book would most likely be massive.' Joanne was also quite happy with the reports that the movie version of *Harry Potter and the Prisoner of Azkaban* had survived the numerous delays in Glencoe and was now right on schedule for its Summer 2004 release.

With her personal life now very much a priority and the professional pressures of the past couple of years behind her, Joanne has emerged a complete, fulfilled woman who continues to make it her mission to bring the joys of Harry Potter into the lives of millions.

'Ultimately I need to do this,' she recently told *The Times*. 'I could have stopped writing four years ago and I would have been fine financially. At this point in my life I'm not writing for the money and I could definitely do without the fame. The only point is to satisfy myself now and out of loyalty to the fans. But when I say it's for me, it's also for Harry ... and being true to what I know will be his end.'

15

HOW ROWLING WRITES

JK Rowling has a simple rule when it comes to sitting down to write her latest adventure of *Harry Potter*: 'I write any time, any place, and in longhand.'

Joanne has often said that it takes her about a year to write a *Harry Potter* book. She has said that a key to turning out a full-length book in that period of time is to be consistent.

'I write nearly every day. Some days I write for ten or eleven hours. Other days I might only write for three hours. It really depends on how fast the ideas are coming to me.'

Having long ago decided that the Harry Potter books would be a seven-book series, Joanne has each storyline already well plotted before she sits down to write the book. 'I always have a basic plot line. But I like to leave some things to be decided when I write. It's more fun that way.'

Also a lot of fun are the strange-sounding names that Joanne incorporates into her tales. 'Some of the names come from folklore, and many of the names are invented.'

'I also collect unusual names and I take them from all sorts of different places. I remember that I came up with the names of the houses at Hogwarts while flying and ended up writing them on the back of an aeroplane sick bag.'

An increasingly difficult aspect of writing the *Harry Potter* books has been how to bring new readers up to speed on the previous events of the series. Joanne has said that, in *Harry Potter and the Chamber of Secrets*, it was relatively easy to fill new readers in on Harry and his first year at Hogwarts.

'But by the time I reach book five and six, this is going to be much harder,' she has said. 'Maybe what I'll do is just write a preface that says 'Previously in *Harry Potter* …' and tell readers to go back and read books one through four.'

Joanne is often asked by youngsters how they can begin to write. Her first suggestion has always been to read everything and anything to get an idea of how writers write. But when it is time to pick up the pencil, the writer has suggested in many interviews that kids use their own lives as a starting point.

'Start by writing the things that you know. Write about your own experiences and your own feelings. That's what I do.'

About the Author

Marc Shapiro has been a freelance entertainment journalist for more than 25 years, covering film, television and music for a number of national and international newspapers and magazines. He is the author of more than a dozen celebrity biographies, including *Freddie Prinze Jr: The Unofficial Biography*; *Love Story: The Unauthorized Biography of Jennifer Love Hewitt*; and *Lucy Lawless: Warrior Princess*. He lives in Pasadena, California, with his wife Nancy, daughter Rachael, dog Keri, and cats Bad Baby and Chaos.

5